Zaner-Bloser
Handwriting
With a simplified alphabet

WITHDRAWN

Author

Clinton S. Hackney

Contributing Authors

Pamela J. Farris
Janice T. Jones
Linda Leonard Lamme

Zaner-Bloser, Inc., P.O. Box 16764, Columbus, Ohio 43210-6764   3018

Copyright © 1999 Zaner-Bloser, Inc.   ISBN 0-88085-958-X

Developed by Kirchoff/Wohlberg, Inc., in cooperation with Zaner-Bloser Publishers

Printed in the United States of America

98 99 00 01 02 WC 5 4 3 2 1

You already know handwriting is important.
Now take a look at...

NEW SIMPLIFIED
Zaner-Bloser Handwriting

Easier to read!   Easier to write!   Easier to teach!

Zaner-Bloser's new
program is easy to teach.

I see Zaner-Bloser's
alphabet in the books I read.

I like Zaner-Bloser because
it's so easy to write.

ii

You already know handwriting is important, but did you know...

Did You Know...

Annually, the U.S. Postal Service receives 38 million illegibly addressed letters, costing American taxpayers $4 million each year.

—American Demographics, Dec. 1992

Did You Know...

Hundreds of thousands of tax returns are delayed every year because figures, notes, and signatures are illegible.

—Better Handwriting in 30 Days, 1989

Did You Know...

Poor handwriting costs American business $200 million annually.

—American Demographics, Dec. 1992

Zaner-Bloser's CONTINUOUS-STROKE manuscript alphabet

Aa Bb Cc Dd Ee Ff Gg
Oo Pp Qq Rr Ss Tt

Easier to Read

Our vertical manuscript alphabet is like the alphabet kids see every day inside and outside of the classroom. They see it in their school books, in important environmental print like road signs, and in books and cartoons they read for fun.

"[Slanted] manuscript is not only harder to learn than traditional [vertical] print, but it creates substantially more letter recognition errors and causes more letter confusion than does the traditional style."

—Debby Kuhl and Peter Dewitz in a paper presented at the 1994 meeting of the American Educational Research Association

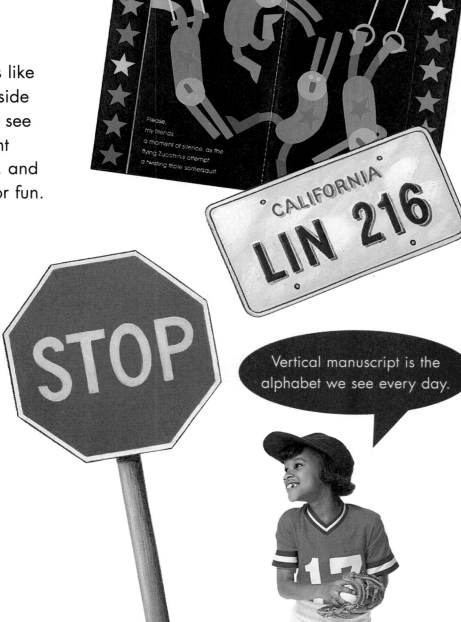

Vertical manuscript is the alphabet we see every day.

CIRCUS by Lois Ehlert ©1992 by Lois Ehlert

Hh Ii Jj Kk Ll Mm Nn
Uu Vv Ww Xx Yy Zz

Easier to Write

Our vertical manuscript alphabet is written with continuous strokes—fewer pencil lifts—so there's a greater sense of flow in writing. And kids can write every letter once they learn four simple strokes that even kindergartners can manage.

Four simple strokes: circle, horizontal line, vertical line, slanted line

"The writing hand has to change direction more often when writing the [slanted] alphabet, do more retracing of lines, and make more strokes that occur later in children's development."

—Steve Graham in *Focus on Exceptional Children*, 1992

Many kids can already write their names when they start school (vertical manuscript).

Kirk

Why should they have to relearn them in another form (slanted manuscript)? With Zaner-Bloser, they don't have to.

Kirk

Easier to Teach

Our vertical manuscript alphabet is easy to teach because there's no reteaching involved. Children are already familiar with our letterforms—they've seen them in their environment and they've learned them at home.

"Before starting school, many children learn how to write traditional [vertical] manuscript letters from their parents or preschool teachers. Learning a special alphabet such as [slanted] means that these children will have to relearn many of the letters they can already write."

—Steve Graham in *Focus on Exceptional Children*, 1992

Zaner-Bloser's NEW SIMPLIFIED cursive alphabet

Aa Bb Cc Dd Ee Ff Gg
Nn Oo Pp Qq Rr Ss

Simplified letterforms... Easier to read and write

old letterform

Letterforms are simplified so they're easier to write and easier to identify in writing. The new simplified **Q** now looks like a **Q** instead of a number 2.

old letterform

Our simplified letterforms use the headline, midline, and baseline as a guide for where letters start and stop. The new simplified **d** touches the headline instead of stopping halfway.

old letterform

No more "cane stems"! Our new simplified letterforms begin with a small curve instead of fancy loops that can be difficult for students to write.

Hh Ii Jj Kk Ll Mm
Tt Uu Vv Ww Xx Yy Zz

Simplified letterforms...
Easier to teach

When handwriting is easy for students to write, instruction time is cut way back! That's the teaching advantage with Zaner-Bloser Handwriting. Our cursive letterforms are simplified so instead of spending a lot of time teaching fancy loops that give kids trouble, teachers give instruction for simple, basic handwriting that students can use for the rest of their lives.

And remember, with Zaner-Bloser Handwriting, students learn to write manuscript with continuous strokes. That means that when it's time for those students to begin writing cursive, the transition comes naturally because they already know the flow of continuous strokes.

These simple letters are so much easier to teach!

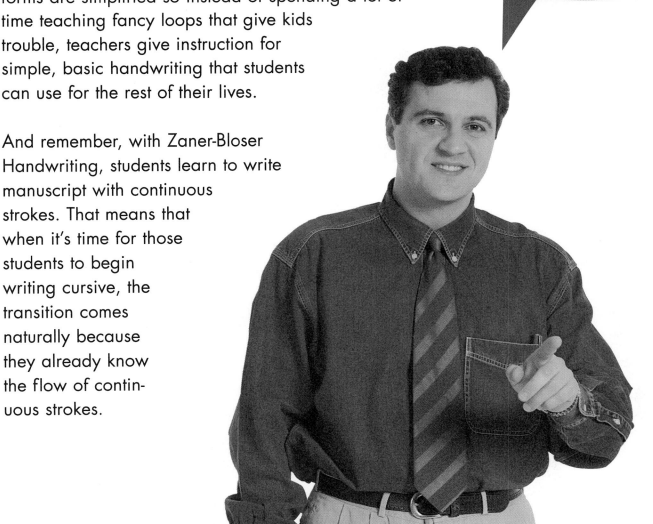

The Student Edition...set up for student success

Letters are grouped and taught by the strokes used to form them.

Students are given ample space for plenty of writing practice.

Helpful hints assist students in avoiding common handwriting problems.

Correct letter models are easy to locate and identify.

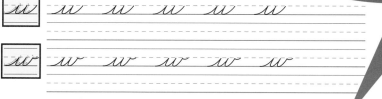

Write Undercurve Letters

Find an undercurve ⟋ in each letter. Write the letters.

Be careful not to loop back. Write:

i not *ei*   *t* not *tt*
u not *ee*   *w* not *eee*

✓Check your writing folder. Do you write these letters without loops?   Yes   No

YOUR PERSONAL BEST

Write the letters one more time.

14

Grade 4 Student Edition

Prewriting · Drafting · Revising · Editing · Publishing

Students are taught the relationship between handwriting and the writing process through activities like this one. Here, students use each step of the writing process to produce an article for a class magazine.

Write for a Class Magazine

A class magazine is a great place for sharing things that interest you and your classmates. It may include different kinds of writing.

Follow these suggestions for putting together a class magazine.

I. Prewriting

Begin by choosing an assignment that interests you. The list below shows some types of articles you could write. Discuss the list with a partner, then **brainstorm** ideas of your own.

news articles   *poems*
stories   *jokes*
book reviews   *riddles*
magazine reviews

What kind of article will you write? Explain your choice.

74

Now use the form below to **plan** your article. Make sure you will be able to read your notes later.

Notes

Date:

Kind of article:

Subject of my article:

What I already know:

What I need to find out:

Think of an interesting title for your article.
Write it below.

75

After reviewing letters, students practice joinings and write complete words.

Students evaluate their own handwriting in every lesson.

Additional notes help students avoid common problems.

Join letters to *i, t, u, w*.
Notice how you join each pair of letters.

Write the words.

te te te → team

ui ui ui → quick

id id id → idea

to to to → tomorrow

um um → umpire

CHECKSTROKE ALERT

Join *u* and *v* at the midline.

ur ur ur

Write *writing*, not *writing*.

writing

EVALUATE

Circle your best joining. Circle your best word.

15

Grade 4 Student Edition

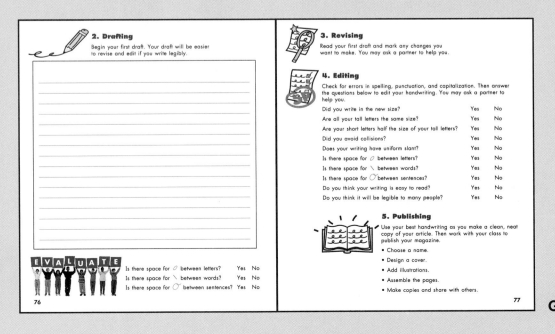

2. Drafting

Begin your first draft. Your draft will be easier to revise and edit if you write legibly.

EVALUATE
Is there space for ○ between letters? Yes No
Is there space for ╲ between words? Yes No
Is there space for ○ between sentences? Yes No

76

3. Revising

Read your first draft and mark any changes you want to make. You may ask a partner to help you.

4. Editing

Check for errors in spelling, punctuation, and capitalization. Then answer the questions below to edit your handwriting. You may ask a partner to help you.

Did you write in the new size? Yes No
Are all your tall letters the same size? Yes No
Are your short letters half the size of your tall letters? Yes No
Did you avoid collisions? Yes No
Does your writing have uniform slant? Yes No
Is there space for ○ between letters? Yes No
Is there space for ╲ between words? Yes No
Is there space for ○ between sentences? Yes No
Do you think your writing is easy to read? Yes No
Do you think it will be legible to many people? Yes No

5. Publishing

Use your best handwriting as you make a clean, neat copy of your article. Then work with your class to publish your magazine.

• Choose a name.
• Design a cover.
• Add illustrations.
• Assemble the pages.
• Make copies and share with others.

77

Grade 4 Student Edition

ix

The Teacher Edition...streamlined instruction

At-a-glance stroke descriptions are short and easy to find.

The student page is close to the instruction for that page.

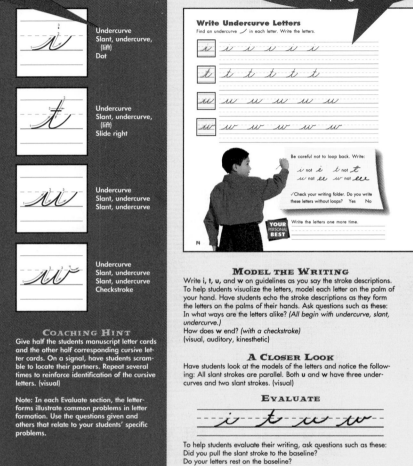

Brief teaching notes save you valuable time.

Undercurve
Slant, undercurve, (lift)
Dot

Undercurve
Slant, undercurve, (lift)
Slide right

Undercurve
Slant, undercurve
Slant, undercurve

Undercurve
Slant, undercurve
Slant, undercurve
Checkstroke

COACHING HINT
Give half the students manuscript letter cards and the other half corresponding cursive letter cards. On a signal, have students scramble to locate their partners. Repeat several times to reinforce identification of the cursive letters. (visual)

Note: In each Evaluate section, the letterforms illustrate common problems in letter formation. Use the questions given and others that relate to your students' specific problems.

14

Write Undercurve Letters
Find an undercurve in each letter. Write the letters.

Be careful not to loop back. Write:

✓Check your writing folder. Do you write these letters without loops? Yes No

YOUR PERSONAL BEST Write the letters one more time.

14

MODEL THE WRITING
Write **i, t, u,** and **w** on guidelines as you say the stroke descriptions. To help students visualize the letters, model each letter on the palm of your hand. Have students echo the stroke descriptions as they form the letters on the palms of their hands. Ask questions such as these: In what ways are the letters alike? *(All begin with undercurve, slant, undercurve.)*
How does **w** end? *(with a checkstroke)*
(visual, auditory, kinesthetic)

A CLOSER LOOK
Have students look at the models of the letters and notice the following: All slant strokes are parallel. Both **u** and **w** have three undercurves and two slant strokes. (visual)

EVALUATE

To help students evaluate their writing, ask questions such as these:
Did you pull the slant stroke to the baseline?
Do your letters rest on the baseline?

Grade 4 Teacher Edition

Language arts connections reinforce writing and other skills.

Join letters to *i, t, u, w.*
Notice how you join each pair of letters.

te	*te*	*te*	*team*
ui	*ui*	*ui*	*quick*
id	*id*	*id*	*idea*
to	*to*	*to*	*tomorrow*
um	*um*		*umpire*

Write the words.

CHECKSTROKE ALERT
Join *u* and *v* at the midline.

wr *wr* *wr*   *writing*

Write *writing,* not ~~*writing.*~~

EVALUATE Circle your best joining. Circle your best word.

15

LETTER JOININGS
Draw students' attention to the undercurve endings of **i, t,** and **u.**
Model how to join these letters to
• an undercurve: **ir, ts, up**
• a downcurve: **ic, ta, ug**
• an overcurve: **ix, ty, uz**
Explain that **w** ends with a checkstroke.
Model how to join **w** to
• an undercurve: **we, ws, wi, wr**
• a downcurve: **wa, wo**
• an overcurve: **wn, wy**
(visual, auditory)

CORRECTIVE STRATEGY

uum NOT *uum*

Slant strokes should be parallel. The undercurve to overcurve joining becomes a doublecurve, but there is no retrace. The doublecurve becomes a part of the following letter.

Corrective strategies offer solutions to common handwriting problems.

Write Away

Ask students to write a paragraph describing their plans for tomorrow. Participate by sharing one of your plans.

PRACTICE MASTER 1

PRACTICE MASTER 2

Practice Masters 79 and 80 provide additional practice.

15

Grade 4 Teacher Edition

Visual references to practice masters for each lesson save you time.

HANDWRITING AND THE WRITING PROCESS

Activities are suggested throughout the Teacher Edition that emphasize the importance of using legible handwriting in all the steps of the writing process.

MAINTAINING MANUSCRIPT

These activities emphasize the need for maintaining good manuscript in many situations throughout life, such as writing envelopes, job applications, test forms, and bank forms.

Grade 4 Practice Masters

An accompanying book of practice masters offers additional practice for every letter and skill students learn. It also includes resources to make teaching easier—certificates, an evaluation record, letters to send home to keep parents and guardians involved, and Spanish activities.

xi

Evaluation and Assessment...
consistent guidance throughout the year

Student self-evaluation...

In every lesson. Students evaluate their own handwriting and circle their best work.

In every review. Several times a year, students review the letterforms and joinings they've learned and again evaluate their handwriting.

Through application activities. Students apply what they've learned in relevant practice activities. In each one, they evaluate their own and others' handwriting.

Teacher assessment...

In every lesson and review. As students evaluate their own writing, teachers can assess their letterforms, as well as their comprehension of good handwriting. Corrective Strategies for each lesson offer teachers helpful hints for common handwriting problems.

Through application activities. Students' work in relevant practice activities offers lots of opportunity for informal assessment of handwriting, language arts, and other areas.

The Keys to Legibility

These four Keys to Legibility are taught and reviewed throughout the program.
They remind students that their goal should be legible handwriting.

Size

Consistently sized letters are easy to read. Students learn to use midlines and headlines to guide the size of their letters.

Slant

Letters with a consistent slant are easy to read. Students learn how to position their papers and hold their pencils so consistent slant comes with ease.

Shape

Four simple strokes—undercurve, downcurve, overcurve, and slant—make it easy for students to write letters with consistent and proper shape.

Spacing

Correct spacing between letters and words makes handwriting easy to read. Practical hints show students how to determine correct spacing.

Handwriting practice...relevant application

On Your Own

Make an address book. Fill out cards for people you know. Punch a hole in each card, arrange the cards in alphabetical order, and string them together.

Fill out the first card. Then write one of your own.

Name: *Paula Stewart*
Address: *3700 Broadway Ave*
Cleveland, OH 43216
Phone Number: *555-5050*
Birthday: *July 9, 1988*
Other Information: *camp friend*

Name: *Danny Jefferson*
Address: *15 Morris Pla*
Austin, TX 7
Phone Number: *555-6912*
Birthday: *February 28,*
Other Information: *cousin*

E V A L U A T E

Are yo
Can yo

**Completed Grade 4
Student Edition**

Students practice their handwriting in relevant ways. Here, they learn how to keep an address book.

On Your Own

Some people keep lists for fun. You might start a list now that you add to for the rest of your life! Here are some ideas of things to keep track of. Check one to try this week, and begin your list below.

☐ license plates   ☐ baseball cards   ☐ foreign cars
☐ books   ☐ funny signs   ☐ new words
☑ birds   ☐ places   ☐ other

sparrow — in yard
blue jay — at feeder
cardinal — at feeder
hawk — in sky
crow — in a field

E V A L U A T E

Can you read your list easily   (Yes)   No
Will you be able to read it   (Yes)   No

49

In this practice activity, students learn how to write lists.

A huge collection of supplementary materials... makes handwriting even easier to teach!

A **Evaluation Guides** *grades 1–6*

B **Poster/Wall Chart Super Pak**
  grades K–6, includes Handwriting Positions Wall Chart, Keys to Legibility Wall Chart, Alphabet Wall Chart, Simplified Stroke Descriptions, and a Portfolio Assessment Guide

C **Story Journals** *grades K–4*

D **Manuscript/Cursive Card Set** *grades 1–6*

E **Sentence Strips** *grades K–6*

F **Writing Journals** *grades 1–6*

G **My ABC Journal** *grades K–1*

H **Pignic Alphabet Book** *grades K–2*

I **From Anne to Zach Alphabet Book** *grades K–2*

J **Letter Cards** *grades K–2*

K **Manuscript/Cursive Fonts**

L **Manuscript Kin-Tac Cards** *grades K–2*

For more information about these materials, call 1-800-421-3018.

M **Make-Your-Own Big Book** *grades K–2*

N **Parent Brochures** *for manuscript/cursive*

O **Book of Transparencies** *grades 1–6*

P **Read, Write, and Color Alphabet Mat** *grades K–2*

Q **Dry Erase Write-On Cards** *grades K–2*

R **Parent/Student Worksheets** *grades 2–6*

S **Peek Thrus** *grades 1–4*

T **Illustrated Alphabet Strips** *grades K–4*

U **Desk Strips** *grades 1–6*

V **Practice Masters** *grades K–6*

W **Alphabet Wall Strips** *grades K–6*

X **Fun With Handwriting** *grades K–8*

Y **Write-On, Wipe-Off Magnetic Board With Letters** *grades K–2*

Z **Post Office Kit** *grades K–4*

Vertical vs. *Slanted* Manuscript

What the research shows

Using a slanted alphabet has been a trend in handwriting instruction. It's actually not a new development—the first slanted alphabet was created in 1968. A sort of bridge between manuscript and cursive, this slanted alphabet used unconnected letterforms like the traditional vertical manuscript, but its letterforms were slanted like cursive.

It seemed like a good idea. This alphabet was to be easier to write than cursive, yet similar enough to cursive that children wouldn't learn two *completely* different alphabets. But after several years of use in some schools, research has uncovered some unfortunate findings.

Slanted manuscript can be difficult to write

Slanted manuscript was created to be similar to cursive, so it uses more complicated strokes such as small curves, and these strokes can be difficult for young children.

Vertical manuscript, on the other hand, is consistent with the development of young children. Each of its letters is formed with simple strokes—straight lines, circles, and slanted lines. One researcher found that the strokes used in vertical manuscript are the same as the shapes children use in their drawings (Farris, 1993). Because children are familiar with these shapes, they can identify and form the strokes with little difficulty.

Slanted manuscript can create problems with legibility

Legibility is an important goal in handwriting. Obviously, content should not be sacrificed for legibility, but what is handwriting if it cannot be read?

Educational researchers have tested the legibility of slanted manuscript and found that children writing vertical manuscript "performed significantly better" than those writing slanted manuscript. The writers of the slanted alphabet tended to make more misshapen letterforms, tended to extend their strokes above and below the guidelines, and had a difficult time keeping their letterforms consistent in size (Graham, 1992).

On the other hand, the vertical manuscript style of print has a lot of support in the area of research. Advertisers have known for years that italic type has a lower readability rate than vertical "roman" type. Research shows that in 30 minute readings, the italic style is read 4.9% slower than roman type (14–16 words per minute). This is why most literature, especially literature for early readers, is published using roman type.

Slanted manuscript can impair letter recognition

Educators have suspected that it would be beneficial for students to write and read the same style of alphabet. In other words, if children *read* vertical manuscript, they should also *write* vertical manuscript. Now it has been found that inconsistent alphabets may actually be detrimental to children's learning.

Researchers have found that slanted manuscript impairs the ability of some young children to recognize many letters. Some children who learn the slanted style alphabet find it difficult to recognize many of the traditional letterforms they see in books and environmental print. "[These children] consistently had difficulty identifying several letters, often making the same erroneous response to the same letter," the researchers reported. They concluded that slanted manuscript "creates substantially more letter recognition errors and causes more letter confusion than does the traditional style." (Kuhl & Dewitz, 1994).

Slanted manuscript does not help with transition

One of the benefits proposed by the creators of the slanted manuscript alphabet was that it made it easier for children to make the transition from manuscript to cursive writing. However, no difference in transition time has been found between the two styles of manuscript alphabets. In addition, the slanted style does not seem to enhance young children's production of cursive letters (Graham, 1992).

"...slanted manuscript letters cannot be recommended as a replacement for the traditional manuscript alphabet."

The slanted style of manuscript appeared to be a good idea. But educators should take a close look at what the research shows before adopting this style of alphabet. As one researcher has said, "Given the lack of supportive evidence and the practical problems involved in implementation, slanted manuscript letters cannot be recommended as a replacement for the traditional manuscript alphabet" (Graham, 1994).

Farris, P.J. (1993). Learning to write the ABC's: A comparison of D'Nealian and Zaner-Bloser handwriting styles. *Indiana Reading Quarterly, 25* (4), 26–33.

Graham, S. (1992). Issues in handwriting instruction. *Focus on Exceptional Children, 25* (2).

Graham, S. (1994, Winter). Are slanted manuscript alphabets superior to the traditional manuscript alphabet? *Childhood Education,* 91–95.

Kuhl, D. & Dewitz, P. (1994, April). The effect of handwriting style on alphabet recognition. Paper presented at the annual meeting of the American Educational Research Association, New Orleans, LA.

Under your care . . .
your students receive the best possible attention everyday!

Now that you use *Zaner-Bloser Handwriting*, we want to be sure you get the attention you need to make your job more successful. We have many communication channels available to meet your needs: phone our Customer Service Department at 1-800-421-3018, visit our website at www.zaner-bloser.com, use the card below to write to our editors, and use the card at the bottom to join our Customer Care Club.

Zaner-Bloser cares!

If you have any questions or comments concerning Zaner-Bloser instructional materials or questions about the teaching of handwriting, you may use this card to write to us. We will be happy to assist you in any way possible.

_____

_____

_____

_____

_____

Ms., Mr., etc.	Name	Position	Grade Level(s)

School	School Address

City	State	ZIP

( )	( )	( )
School Telephone	After Hours Phone	FAX

MH0327

Zaner-Bloser Customer Care Club

Join the Zaner-Bloser Customer Care Club and we'll make sure you stay up-to-date on current educational research and products. To enroll, you may return this card or call our Customer Care Club hotline at 1-800-387-2410. Upon enrollment, we'll get you started with a gift of information about teaching handwriting.

 **YES!** Please enroll me in the Zaner-Bloser Customer Care Club and send me the following pamphlet: **The Left-Handed Child in a Right-Handed World**

Zaner-Bloser

2200 W. Fifth Ave.
PO Box 16764
Columbus, OH
43216-6764

Visit our website:
www.zaner-bloser.com

Ms., Mr., etc.	Name	Position	Grade Level(s)

School	School Address

City	State	ZIP

( )	( )	( )
School Telephone	After Hours Phone	FAX

Please Note: This program is for Zaner-Bloser customers only!

MH0327

Zaner-Bloser

Customer Service: 1-800-421-3018

Customer Care Club: 1-800-387-2410

Website: www.zaner-bloser.com

BUSINESS REPLY MAIL
FIRST CLASS MAIL   PERMIT NO. 295   COLUMBUS, OH

POSTAGE WILL BE PAID BY ADDRESSEE

Zaner-Bloser
2200 W 5TH AVE
PO BOX 16764
COLUMBUS OH 43272-4176

BUSINESS REPLY MAIL
FIRST CLASS MAIL   PERMIT NO. 295   COLUMBUS, OH

POSTAGE WILL BE PAID BY ADDRESSEE

Zaner-Bloser
2200 W 5TH AVE
PO BOX 16764
COLUMBUS OH 43272-4176

Meeting Students' Individual Handwriting Needs

The Left-Handed Student

With proper instruction and encouragement, left-handed students can write as well as right-handed students. Three important techniques assist the left-handed student in writing.

Paper Position

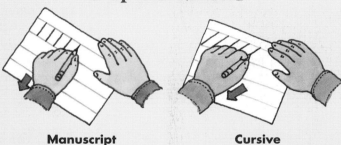

Manuscript   **Cursive**

For *manuscript writing,* the **lower right corner** of the paper should point toward the left of the body's midsection.

For *cursive writing,* the **lower right corner** of the paper should point toward the body's midsection.

Downstrokes are pulled toward the left elbow.

Pencil Position

The top of the pencil should point toward the left elbow. The pen or pencil should be held at least one inch above the point. This allows students to see what they are writing.

Arm Position

Holding the left arm close to the body and keeping the hand below the line of writing prevents "hooking" the wrist and smearing the writing.

Students With Reversal Tendencies

- Downcurve
- Undercurve
- Slant
- Loop forward, undercurve

Directionality

A problem with directionality (moving from left to right across the page) interferes with a child's ability to form letters correctly and to write text that makes sense. To develop correct directionality, try these techniques:

- Provide opportunities for the child to write at the chalkboard within a confined area with frequent arrows as a reminder of left-to-right progression.
- Prepare sheets of paper on which the left edges and the beginning stroke of a letter, such as *b,* are colored green.

Letter Reversals

Determine which letters a student most often reverses. Make a list of these reversals and concentrate on them either on an individual basis or by grouping together the students who are reversing the same letters.

- Emphasize each step of the stroke description before the children write a letter.
- Provide a letter for tracing that has been colored according to stroke order. Repeat the stroke description with the children as they write the letter.
- Encourage the children to write the letter as they verbalize the stroke description.

Students With Other Special Needs

Success in handwriting is almost always a certainty if the initial instruction involves visual, auditory, and kinesthetic stimuli—a multisensory approach. Students need to develop a correct mental and motor image of the stroke, joining, letter, or word before they attempt to write. These techniques may help your students with special needs.

For the Kinesthetic Learner

- Walk out the letter strokes on the floor.
- Form letters in the air using full-arm movement.
- Make letter models with clay or string.
- Write strokes, letters, and joinings in sand.
- Use different writing instruments, such as crayons, markers, and varied sizes of pencils.
- Trace large strokes, letters, and joinings on the chalkboard and on paper—first with fingers, then with chalk or other media.
- Dip fingers in water and form letters and joinings on the chalkboard.

Remember that initial instruction, remediation, and maintenance for the student whose primary sensory modality is kinesthetic should be tactile, involving movement and the sense of touch.

For the Auditory Learner

- Verbalize each stroke in the letter as that letter is presented.
- Encourage the student to verbalize the letter strokes and to explain how strokes are alike and how they are different in the letterforms.
- Ask students to write random letters as you verbalize the strokes.
- Be consistent in the language you use to describe letters, strokes, shapes, and joinings.

Students whose primary sensory modality is auditory require instruction that enables them to listen and to verbalize.

For the Visual Learner

- Encourage students first to look at the letter as a whole and to ask themselves if the letter is tall or short, fat or skinny. Does all of the letter rest on the baseline, or is it a descender or a tall letter? How many and what kinds of strokes are in the letter?
- Have students look at each individual stroke carefully before they attempt to write the letter.

As a general rule, a student whose primary sensory modality is visual will have little difficulty in handwriting if instruction includes adequate visual stimuli.

For Learners With Attention Deficit Problems

Because they have difficulty focusing and maintaining attention, these students must concentrate on individual strokes in the letterforms. When they have learned the strokes, they can put them together to form letters, and then learn the joinings (in cursive) to write words.

- Give very short assignments.
- Supervise closely and give frequent encouragement.

Activities recommended for kinesthetic learners are appropriate for students with an attention deficit disorder.

General Coaching Tips for Teachers

- Teach a handwriting lesson daily, if possible, for no more than 15 minutes. Short, daily periods of instruction are preferable to longer, but less frequent, periods.
- Surround children with models of good handwriting. Set an example when you write on the chalkboard and on students' papers.
- Teach the letters through basic strokes.
- Emphasize one key to legibility at a time.
- Use appropriately ruled paper. Don't be afraid to increase the size of the grids for any student who is experiencing difficulty.
- Stress comfortable writing posture and pencil position. Increase the size of the pencil for students who "squeeze" the writing implement.
- Show the alternate method of holding the pencil, and allow students to choose the one that is better for them. (Refer to the alternate method shown on the Position Pages in the Teacher Edition.)
- Provide opportunities for children in the upper grades to use manuscript writing. Permit manuscript for some assignments, if children prefer manuscript to cursive.
- Encourage students with poor sustained motor control to use conventional manuscript, with frequent lifts, if continuous manuscript is difficult for them.

Zaner-Bloser
Handwriting
With a simplified alphabet

Author
Clinton S. Hackney

Contributing Authors
Pamela J. Farris
Janice T. Jones
Linda Leonard Lamme

Zaner-Bloser, Inc.
P.O. Box 16764
Columbus, Ohio 43216-6764

Teacher Edition Artists:

Diane Blasius; Lizi Boyd; Denise & Fernando;
Tom Leonard;
Daniel Moreton; Diane Paterson

Photos:

John Lei

Author
Clinton S. Hackney, Ed.D.

Contributing Authors
Pamela J. Farris, Ph.D.
Janice T. Jones, M.A.
Linda Leonard Lamme, Ph.D.

Reviewers

Judy L. Bausch, Columbus, Georgia
Cherlynn Bruce, Conroe, Texas
Karen H. Burke, Director of Curriculum and Instruction, Bar Mills, Maine
Anne Chamberlin, Lynchburg, Virginia
Carol J. Fuhler, Flagstaff, Arizona
Deborah D. Gallagher, Gainesville, Florida
Kathleen Harrington, Redford, Michigan
Rebecca James, East Greenbush, New York
Gerald R. Maeckelbergh, Principal, Blaine, Minnesota
Bessie B. Peabody, Principal, East St. Louis, Illinois

Marilyn S. Petruska, Coraopolis, Pennsylvania
Sharon Ralph, Nashville, Tennessee
Linda E. Ritchie, Birmingham, Alabama
Roberta Hogan Royer, North Canton, Ohio
Marion Redmond Starks, Baltimore, Maryland
Elizabeth J. Taglieri, Lake Zurich, Illinois
Claudia Williams, Lewisburg, West Virginia

Credits

Art: Liz Callen: 31, 72; Denise & Fernando: 3, 5, 12, 26, 35, 46, 56, 66; David Diaz: 1, 4, 51, 54, 61; Gloria Elliott: 5, 12, 26, 46, 56, 66; Oki Han: 62–63; Rosekrans Hoffman: 3, 29, 41, 68; Tom Leonard: 4, 33, 37, 39, 49, 64; Daniel Moreton: 68–71, 74–77; Sarah Snow: 43, 45, 55

Photos: John Lei/OPC: 7–9, 13, 15, 17, 19, 21, 23–25, 27–29, 31, 33, 35, 37, 39, 41, 43, 45, 47–53, 55, 57–64, 67–71, 73–78; Stephen Ogilvy: 4, 11, 14, 16, 30, 32, 34, 36, 38, 40, 42, 44, 74

Literature: "It's Dark In Here" from *Where The Sidewalk Ends* by Shel Silverstein. Copyright © 1974 by Evil Eye Music, Inc.

Developed by Kirchoff/Wohlberg, Inc., in cooperation with Zaner-Bloser Publishers
Cover illustration by David Diaz

ISBN 0-88085-949-0

Copyright © 1999 Zaner-Bloser, Inc.

CONTENTS

Unit 1 Getting Started

Unit 2 Writing Lowercase Letters
Handwriting Emphasis: Size and Shape

Unit 3 Writing Uppercase Letters
Handwriting Emphasis: Size and Shape

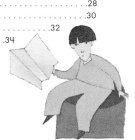

Unit 4 Writing for Yourself
Handwriting Emphasis: Smaller Size

Unit 5 Writing for Someone Else
Handwriting Emphasis: Slant

Unit 6 Writing for Publication
Handwriting Emphasis: Spacing

I wrote down what I need for the cookout.

Do you think Tim is really supposed to take lions to the cookout? But what is he supposed to take? You have probably guessed that Tim's handwriting is hard even for him to read. Let's hope his mother figures out he meant to write *beans*, not *lions*.

The lessons in this book will help you write legibly so you and other people can read what you have written.

You will learn how correct letter size and shape, uniform slant, and correct spacing make your writing easy to read.

5

PRACTICE MASTERS FOR UNIT 1

- Letter to Parents—English, 35
- Letter to Parents—Spanish, 36
- Alphabet—English, 39
- Alphabet—Spanish, 40
- Record of Student's Handwriting Skills, 31
- Zaner-Bloser Handwriting Grid, 77

M MAINTAINING MANUSCRIPT

Permit students to use manuscript for creative writing, spelling assignments, and tests if they choose to do so.

Give a weekly assignment that requires manuscript, such as filling out forms, map study, charts, preparing labels and captions, crossword puzzles, and making posters.

Use manuscript on the chalkboard for various purposes, especially vocabulary and dictionary study, as well as other work involving word attack skills.

UNIT SUMMARY

This page tells students about the content, organization, and focus of the book. Students get started by taking a pretest to assess current ability. The lessons that follow review what students need to know to develop good handwriting skills.

PREVIEW THE BOOK

Preview the book with students, calling attention to its organization.

- Unit 1 presents handwriting basics.
- Unit 2 introduces lowercase cursive letters grouped by common strokes.
- Unit 3 introduces uppercase cursive letters grouped by common strokes.
- Units 4–6 provide a variety of opportunities for students to write for different audiences.

Point out that students will evaluate their handwriting frequently. Set up a portfolio for each student to assess individual progress throughout the year.

You may have students use the first five lines of the poem on page 6 as a model for writing on page 7. Or you might ask students to write their favorite lines from this poem. Remind them to use correct letter size and shape, uniform slant, and correct spacing as they write. Be sure to have students save whatever they write for the pretest in their books or writing portfolios so that they can compare the same thing for the posttest later in the year. (visual, kinesthetic)

6

Pretest

It's Dark in Here
by Shel Silverstein

I am writing these poems
From inside a lion.
And it's rather dark in here.
So please excuse the handwriting
Which may not be too clear.
But this afternoon by the lion's cage
I'm afraid I got too near.
And I'm writing these lines
From inside a lion.
And it's rather dark in here.

6

Write the first five lines of this poem in your best cursive handwriting.

E V A L U A T E

Do your tall letters touch the headline?   Yes   No

Do your short letters touch the midline?   Yes   No

Do your letters slant the same way?   Yes   No

Is your spacing correct?   Yes   No

7

EVALUATE

As students write, monitor and informally assess their performance. Then guide them through the self-evaluation process. Meet individually with students to help them assess their handwriting. Ask them how they would like to improve their writing. (visual, auditory)

COACHING HINT: SELF-EVALUATION

Self-evaluation is an important step in the handwriting process. By identifying their own strengths and weaknesses, students become independent learners.

The self-evaluation process steps are as follows:

1. Question

Students should ask themselves questions, such as: "Is my slant correct?" "Does my letter rest on the baseline?"

2. Compare

Students should compare their handwriting to correct models.

3. Evaluate

Students should determine the strengths and weaknesses in their handwriting based on the keys to legibility.

4. Diagnose

Students should diagnose the cause of any difficulties. Possible causes include incorrect paper or pencil position, inconsistent pressure on pencil, and improper strokes.

5. Improve

Self-evaluation should include a means of improvement through additional instruction and continued practice. (visual, auditory, kinesthetic)

LEFT-HANDED WRITERS
RIGHT-HANDED WRITERS

Suggest that students refer to these pages throughout the year as a reminder of proper posture and correct paper and pencil position. Demonstrate correct positions for both left-handed and right-handed writers. Then ask students to place a sheet of paper in the proper position on their desks, pick up a pencil, and write their names. (visual, auditory, kinesthetic)

COACHING HINT

You may wish to group left-handed students together for instruction if you can do so without calling attention to the practice. They should be seated to the left of the chalkboard.

See the Handwriting Positions Wall Chart for more information.

If you are left-handed . . .

Sit up tall. Place both arms on the table. Keep your feet flat on the floor. This way, your body will be well balanced.

Hold your pencil with your first two fingers and thumb. Point the pencil toward your left elbow.

Your paper should slant with the lower right corner pointing toward you. Pull your downstrokes toward your left elbow. Then you can make your writing slant the way you want it to.

Left-Handed Writers

8

PENCIL POSITION

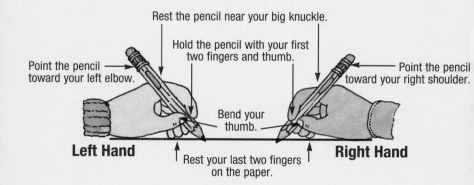

Rest the pencil near your big knuckle.

Hold the pencil with your first two fingers and thumb.

Point the pencil toward your left elbow.

Point the pencil toward your right shoulder.

Bend your thumb.

Left Hand

Rest your last two fingers on the paper.

Right Hand

PAPER POSITION

Left Hand

Right Hand

Right-Handed Writers

If you are right-handed . . .

Sit up tall. Place both arms on the table. Keep your feet flat on the floor. This way, your body will be well balanced.

Hold your pencil with your first two fingers and thumb. Point the pencil toward your right shoulder.

Your paper should slant with the lower left corner pointing toward you. Pull your downstrokes toward your midsection. Then you can make your writing slant the way you want it to.

9

EVALUATE
Check for correct paper and pencil position. The Zaner-Bloser Writing Frame can be used to improve hand position. (visual, kinesthetic)

COACHING HINT: USE OF THE CHALKBOARD

You and your students can follow these suggestions for writing on the chalkboard.

Left-hander. Stand in front of the writing lines and pull the downstrokes to the left elbow. The elbow is bent, and the writing is done at a comfortable height. Step to the right often to maintain correct slant.

Right-hander. Stand to the left of the writing lines and pull the downstrokes toward the midsection of the body. The elbow is bent, and the writing is done at a comfortable height. Step to the right often to maintain correct slant. (visual, kinesthetic)

Students who have difficulty with the traditional pencil position may prefer the alternate method of holding the pencil between the first and second fingers.

CURSIVE LETTERS AND NUMERALS

Students can use the chart at the top of the page to review cursive letters and numerals. (visual, auditory)

COACHING HINT

Review with students the use of guidelines for correct letter formation. Draw guidelines on the chalkboard, using colored chalk to identify the headline, midline, and baseline. Invite volunteers to write words on the guidelines. (visual, auditory, kinesthetic)

Cursive Letters and Numerals

Aa Bb Cc Dd Ee Ff Gg
Hh Ii Jj Kk Ll Mm
Nn Oo Pp Qq Rr Ss Tt
Uu Vv Ww Xx Yy Zz
1 2 3 4 5 6 7 8 9 10

Write your initials and the initials of a friend.

Write the lowercase letters you think you use most.

Write your area code and your ZIP code.

Write your name.

Write the letters and numerals you want to improve.

10

EVALUATE

Poll students to find out which letters and numerals are most difficult for them to write. Discuss why. (auditory, kinesthetic)

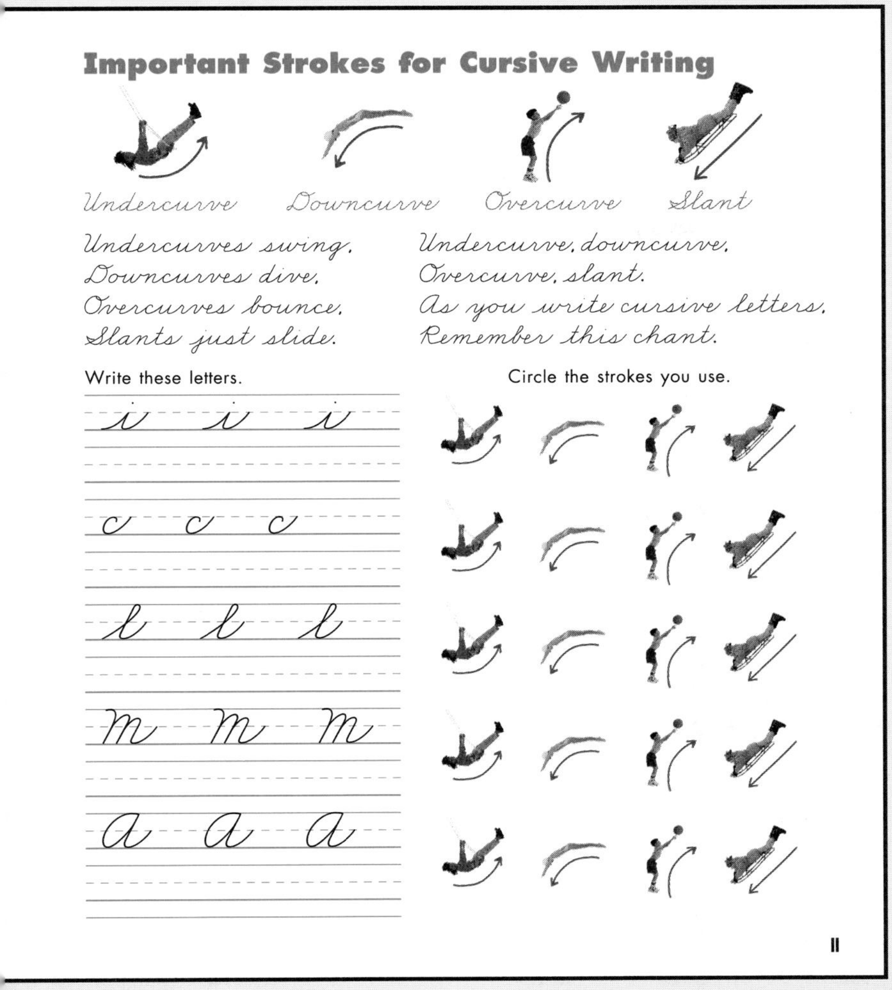
Important Strokes for Cursive Writing

Undercurve Downcurve Overcurve Slant

Undercurves swing.
Downcurves dive.
Overcurves bounce.
Slants just slide.

Undercurve, downcurve,
Overcurve, slant.
As you write cursive letters,
Remember this chant.

Write these letters.

i i i
c c c
l l l
m m m
a a a

Circle the strokes you use.

11

Model the Writing

Model the two sizes of each stroke on guidelines. Invite students to say the names as they write the strokes in the air. Point out that cursive letters are formed from these basic strokes. Suggest students name the strokes as they write each letter to complete the page. (visual, auditory, kinesthetic)

Important Strokes for Cursive Writing

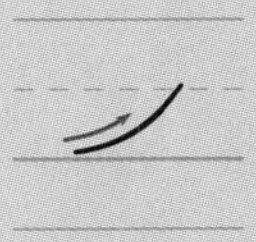

UNDERCURVE
Touch the baseline; curve under and up to the midline.

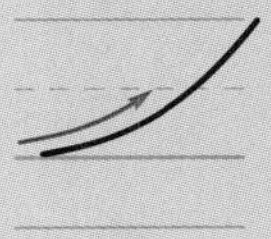

UNDERCURVE
Touch the baseline; curve under and up to the headline.

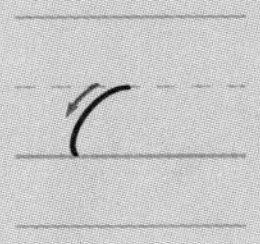

DOWNCURVE
Touch the midline; curve left and down to the baseline.

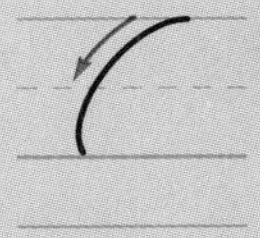

DOWNCURVE
Touch the headline; curve left and down to the baseline.

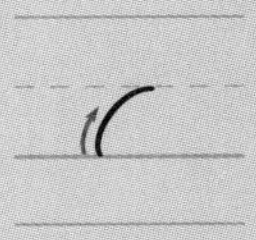

OVERCURVE
Touch the baseline; curve up and right to the midline.

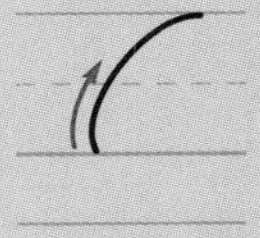

OVERCURVE
Touch the baseline; curve up and right to the headline.

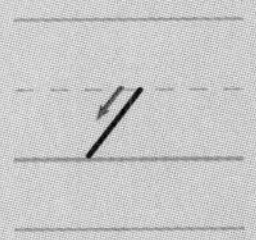

SLANT
Touch the midline; slant left to the baseline.

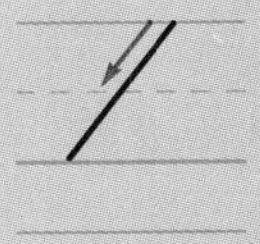

SLANT
Touch the headline; slant left to the baseline.

Before You Go On . . . .

Say it in cursive.

Writing Lowercase Letters

Write the lowercase cursive alphabet.

To write legibly in cursive, you must form and join lowercase letters correctly. The lessons in this unit will show you how. In the following pages, you will write lowercase letters grouped by common strokes. As you write, you will focus on size and shape to help make your writing legible.

12

UNIT SUMMARY

This page tells students about the content, organization, and focus of the unit. Then students are introduced to the first two keys to legibility for lowercase letters: size and shape. The lessons that follow emphasize lowercase letter formation and joinings. Evaluations focus on letter size and shape.

PREVIEW THE UNIT

Preview the unit with students, calling attention to these features:

- letter models with numbered directional arrows
- guidelines for student writing directly beneath handwriting models
- hints about common handwriting problems
- opportunities for students to check their writing folders (or any outside writing) for common handwriting problems
- hints about joining lowercase letters
- opportunities to write letters independently after practice
- opportunities to evaluate letter size and shape

Keys to Legibility: Size and Shape

Lowercase letters are formed from these strokes. Write the strokes.

undercurve	downcurve	overcurve	slant

Tall letters touch the headline. Write these tall letters.

b d f h k l t

Short letters touch the midline. Write these short letters.

a c e g i j m n o p

q r s u v w x y z

Letters with descenders go below the baseline. Write these letters.

f g j p q y z

EVALUATE

Compare your letters with the models.
Are they the same size and shape?   Yes   No

13

MODEL THE WRITING

Write the basic strokes on guidelines as you name each stroke. Invite students to say the names as they write the strokes in the air. Point out that lowercase cursive letters are formed from these basic strokes. Then model writing a tall letter, a short letter, and a letter with a descender, noting the placement of each letter on the guidelines. Remind students that all letters of the same size should be the same height. (visual, auditory, kinesthetic)

EVALUATE

Guide students through the self-evaluation process. Then ask them if they can read their letters easily. Encourage them to explain why or why not. (visual, auditory)

HANDWRITING AND THE WRITING PROCESS

Throughout this unit, questions preceded by a red check mark will prompt students to go to their writing folders and check for common handwriting problems. If cumulative folders are not available, students may evaluate any written work (including homework papers, tests, and creative writing assignments).

You may wish to take these opportunities to remind students that legible handwriting is important in all subject areas. Getting into the habit of evaluating handwriting as a regular part of the editing stage of the writing process will help students maintain their handwriting skills.

Undercurve
Slant, undercurve,
(lift)
Dot

Undercurve
Slant, undercurve,
(lift)
Slide right

Undercurve
Slant, undercurve
Slant, undercurve

Undercurve
Slant, undercurve
Slant, undercurve
Checkstroke

COACHING HINT

Give half the students manuscript letter cards and the other half corresponding cursive letter cards. On a signal, have students scramble to locate their partners. Repeat several times to reinforce identification of the cursive letters. (visual)

Note: In each Evaluate section, the letterforms illustrate common problems in letter formation. Use the questions given and others that relate to your students' specific problems.

14

Write Undercurve Letters

Find an undercurve ⟋ in each letter. Write the letters.

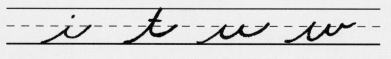

Be careful not to loop back. Write:

i not *e*   *t* not *t*
u not *ee*   *w* not *eee*

✓Check your writing folder. Do you write these letters without loops?   Yes   No

YOUR PERSONAL BEST   Write the letters one more time.

14

MODEL THE WRITING

Write **i, t, u,** and **w** on guidelines as you say the stroke descriptions. To help students visualize the letters, model each letter on the palm of your hand. Have students echo the stroke descriptions as they form the letters on the palms of their hands. Ask questions such as these: In what ways are the letters alike? *(All begin with undercurve, slant, undercurve.)*
How does **w** end? *(with a checkstroke)*
(visual, auditory, kinesthetic)

A CLOSER LOOK

Have students look at the models of the letters and notice the following: All slant strokes are parallel. Both **u** and **w** have three undercurves and two slant strokes. (visual)

EVALUATE

i   t   u   w

To help students evaluate their writing, ask questions such as these:
Did you pull the slant stroke to the baseline?
Do your letters rest on the baseline?

Join letters to *i, t, u, w*.

Notice how you join each pair of letters.   Write the words.

te   te   te →   *team*

ui   ui   ui →   *quick*

id   id   id →   *idea*

to   to   to →   *tomorrow*

um   um →   *umpire*

CHECKSTROKE
ALERT

Join *w* and *v* at the midline.   Write *writing*,
not *writing*.

wr   wr   wr   *writing*

E V A L U A T E   Circle your best joining. Circle your best word.

15

LETTER JOININGS

Draw students' attention to the undercurve endings of **i**, **t**, and **u**.
Model how to join these letters to

- an undercurve: **ir, ts, up**
- a downcurve: **ic, ta, ug**
- an overcurve: **ix, ty, uz**

Explain that **w** ends with a checkstroke.
Model how to join **w** to

- an undercurve: **we, ws, wi, wr**
- a downcurve: **wa, wo**
- an overcurve: **wn, wy**

(visual, auditory)

CORRECTIVE STRATEGY

uw   **NOT**   *uw*

Slant strokes should be parallel. The undercurve to overcurve joining becomes a doublecurve, but there is no retrace. The doublecurve becomes a part of the following letter.

Ask students to write a paragraph describing their plans for tomorrow. Participate by sharing one of your plans.

Name

Write.

i   i   i   t   t   t

u   u   u   w   w   w

ti   ti   ti   until

ud   ud   ud   studies

in   in   in   minute

CHECKSTROKE ALERT

we   we   we   answer

wo   wo   wo   wooden

EVALUATE Circle your best letter. Circle your best word.
Copyright © Zaner-Bloser, Inc.   PRACTICE MASTER 1

PRACTICE MASTER 1

Name

Write.

tu   tu   tu   altitude

ic   ic   ic   picnic

um   um   um   around

CHECKSTROKE ALERT

wd   wd   wd   crowd

a crowded picnic

at a lower altitude

around and about

EVALUATE Circle your best joining. Circle your best word.
PRACTICE MASTER 2   Copyright © Zaner-Bloser, Inc.

PRACTICE MASTER 2

Practice Masters 79 and 80 provide additional practice.

15

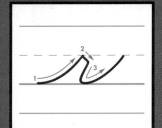

Undercurve
Slant right
Slant, undercurve

Undercurve
**Retrace, curve
  down and back**
Undercurve

Undercurve
Slant, loop back
**Overcurve, curve
  back**
Undercurve

Undercurve
Slant
**Loop back, over-
  curve, (lift)**
Dot

Write Undercurve Letters

Find an undercurve ⟋ in each letter. Write the letters.

Don't round *r*. Remember to close
s, *p*, and *j*. Write:

r not *n*   *s* not *o*
p not *p*   *j* not *g*

✓Check your writing folder. Do you write
these letters correctly?   Yes   No

Write the letters one more time.

YOUR PERSONAL BEST

16

MODEL THE WRITING

Write **r, s, p,** and **j** on guidelines as you say the stroke descriptions.
To help students visualize the letters, model each letter in the air. Have
students echo the stroke descriptions as they form the letters in the air.
Ask questions such as these:
Which letters begin and end with an undercurve? *(r, s, p)*
How does **j** end? *(with an overcurve)*
(visual, auditory, kinesthetic)

A CLOSER LOOK

Have students look at the models of the letters and notice the following: The bottom of **s** is closed; **r** is not. The descenders of **p** and **j** loop
back. *(visual)*

EVALUATE

To help students evaluate their writing, ask questions such as these:
Do your beginning undercurves end at the midline?
Did you close your loops at the baseline?

Join letters to *r, s, p, j.*
Notice how you join each pair of letters.   Write the words.

se   se   se → *separate*

ju   ju   ju → *judge*

ro   ro   ro → *rough*

sm   sm   sm → *smooth*

ry   ry   ry → *diary*

JOINING ALERT

Notice the doublecurve *s*.   Write *packages,*
                                     not *packages*.

pa   pa   pa   *packages*

EVALUATE Circle your best joining. Circle your best word.

LETTER JOININGS

Draw students' attention to the undercurve endings of **r, s,** and **p.**
Model how to join these letters to

- an undercurve: **ri, st, pl**
- a downcurve: **rd, sa, po**
- an overcurve: **rv, sn, py**

Point out that **j** ends with an overcurve.
Model how to join **j** to

- an undercurve: **je, ji, ju**
- a downcurve: **ja, jo**

(visual, auditory)

CORRECTIVE STRATEGY

pa   **NOT**   *pa*

The undercurve to downcurve joining becomes a doublecurve. At the
end of the doublecurve, you retrace. The retrace ends about halfway
between the midline and baseline.

Write Away

Ask students to write a diary entry
describing highlights of their day yes-
terday. Participate by describing something interesting you did.

COACHING HINT

To stress correct joining strokes, ask
students to write any word on the
chalkboard, then use colored chalk to
highlight the joining strokes. (visual,
kinesthetic)

Name _____

Write.

v   v   v   s   s   s

p   p   p   j   j   j

si   si   si   prize

pa   pa   pa   parent

sm   sm   sm   smiling

je   je   je   jealous

jo   jo   jo   enjoys

EVALUATE Circle your best letter. Circle your best word.

Copyright © Zaner-Bloser, Inc.   PRACTICE MASTER 3

PRACTICE MASTER 3

Name _____

Write.

si   si   si   simple

po   po   po   potatoes

sm   sm   sm   farmer

ji   ji   ji   jingle

ja   ja   ja   jade

a prize potato

a happy jingle

EVALUATE Circle your best joining. Circle your best word.

PRACTICE MASTER 4   Copyright © Zaner-Bloser, Inc.

PRACTICE MASTER 4

*Practice Masters 81 and 82 provide
additional practice.*

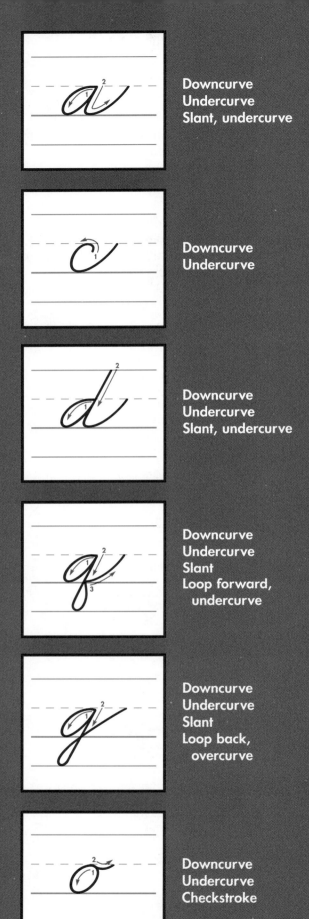

Downcurve
Undercurve
Slant, undercurve

Downcurve
Undercurve

Downcurve
Undercurve
Slant, undercurve

Downcurve
Undercurve
Slant
Loop forward,
 undercurve

Downcurve
Undercurve
Slant
Loop back,
 overcurve

Downcurve
Undercurve
Checkstroke

Write Downcurve Letters

Find a downcurve ⌒ in each letter. Write the letters.

a   a   a   a   a   a   a

c   c   c   c   c   c

d   d   d   d   d   d

a   a   a   a   a   a

g   g   g   g   g   g

o   o   o   o   o   o

YOUR PERSONAL BEST

Write the letters one more time.

Don't loop *c*. Close *a, d, q, g,* and *o*.
Write: *a* not *cɑ*   *c* not *e*
 d not *cl*   *q* not *cf*
 g not *cy*   *o* not *cv*

✓Check your writing folder. Do you close letters that should be closed?   Yes   No

18

MODEL THE WRITING

Write **a, c, d, q, g,** and **o** on guidelines as you say the stroke descriptions. To help students visualize the letters, model each letter on the chalkboard. Have students echo the stroke descriptions as they form the letters on their desks. Ask questions such as these:
How does **g** differ from **q**? *(While g loops back and ends with an overcurve, q loops forward and ends with an undercurve.)*
How does **o** end? *(with a checkstroke)*
(visual, auditory, kinesthetic)

A CLOSER LOOK

Have students look at the models of the letters and notice the following: The letters **a, c, d, q, g,** and **o** begin just below the midline.
(visual)

EVALUATE

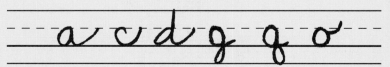

To help students evaluate their writing, ask questions such as these:
Do your letters slant forward?
Do your letters end at the midline?

Join letters to *a, c, d, q, g, o.*

Notice how you join each pair of letters.   Write the words.

di   di   di →   *discover*

qu   qu   qu →   *quiet*

ac   ac   ac →   *accept*

cy   cy   cy →   *recycle*

go   go   go →   *good-bye*

CHECKSTROKE ALERT

Join *o* and *x* at the midline.   Write *oxen*, not *axen*.

ox   ox   ox   *oxen*

E V A L U A T E   Circle your best joining. Circle your best word.

19

LETTER JOININGS

Draw students' attention to the undercurve endings of **a, c, d,** and **q**.
Model how to join these letters to

- an undercurve: **ab, cl, de, qu**
- a downcurve: **aq, co, dd**
- an overcurve: **ax, cy, dy**

Point out that **g** ends with an overcurve.
Model how to join **g** to

- an undercurve: **gh, gl, gu**
- a downcurve: **ga, go**
- an overcurve: **gn, gy**

Explain that **o** ends with a checkstroke.
Model how to join **o** to

- an undercurve: **of, op, or, ot**
- a downcurve: **oa, od, og, oo**
- an overcurve: **om, on, ox, oz**

(visual, auditory)

CORRECTIVE STRATEGY

qu   **NOT**   *qu*

Close the loop at the baseline.

Ask students to write a paragraph about recycling. Participate by describing items you recycle.

COACHING HINT

Remind students that a little more space is needed before words that begin with a downcurve letter (**a, c, d, q, g,** and **o**). Write a sentence on the chalkboard. Use colored chalk to indicate the space needed. (visual, auditory)

Name

Write.
a   a   a   c   c   c

d   d   d   q   q   q

g   g   g   o   o   o

qu   qu   qu   square

da   da   da   darkness

gh   gh   gh   laugh

CHECKSTROKE ALERT
oo   oo   oo   cool

EVALUATE Circle your best letter. Circle your best word.
Copyright © Zaner-Bloser, Inc.   **PRACTICE MASTER 5**

PRACTICE MASTER 5

Name

Write.
cl   cl   cl   clue

an   an   an   company

go   go   go   goose

CHECKSTROKE ALERT
ou   ou   ou   thousand

silly goose

a thousand laughs

part company

EVALUATE Circle your best joining. Circle your best word.
PRACTICE MASTER 6   Copyright © Zaner-Bloser, Inc.

PRACTICE MASTER 6

Practice Masters 83, 84, and 85 provide additional practice.

19

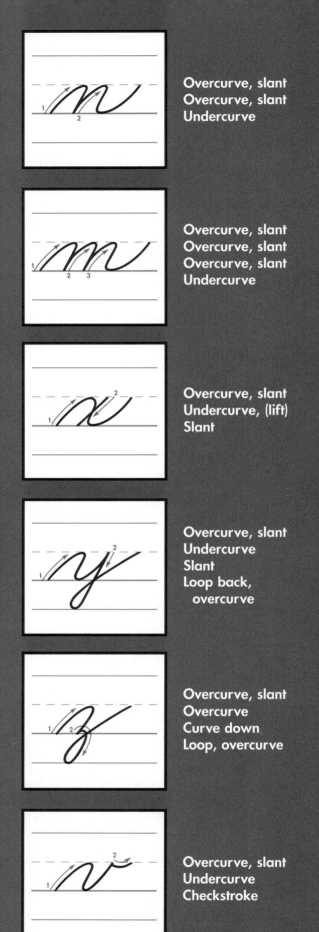

Overcurve, slant
Overcurve, slant
Undercurve

Overcurve, slant
Overcurve, slant
Overcurve, slant
Undercurve

Overcurve, slant
Undercurve, (lift)
Slant

Overcurve, slant
Undercurve
Slant
Loop back,
  overcurve

Overcurve, slant
Overcurve
Curve down
Loop, overcurve

Overcurve, slant
Undercurve
Checkstroke

20

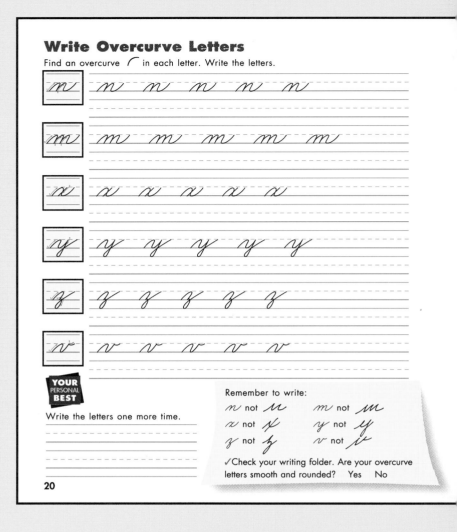

Write Overcurve Letters
Find an overcurve ⌢ in each letter. Write the letters.

YOUR PERSONAL BEST

Write the letters one more time.

Remember to write:

n not *u*　*m* not *w*
x not *x*　*y* not *y*
z not *z*　*v* not *v*

✓Check your writing folder. Are your overcurve letters smooth and rounded?　Yes　No

20

MODEL THE WRITING
Write **n, m, x, y, z,** and **v** on guidelines as you say the stroke descriptions. To help students visualize the letters, model each letter on the palm of your hand. Have students echo the stroke descriptions as they form the letters on the palms of their hands. Ask questions such as these:
How do all the letters begin? *(with overcurve, slant)*
How does **v** end? *(with a checkstroke)*
(visual, auditory, kinesthetic)

A CLOSER LOOK
Have students look at the models of the letters and notice the following: There are two overcurve, slant strokes in **n** and three overcurve, slant strokes in **m**. Both **y** and **z** end with an overcurve. *(visual)*

EVALUATE

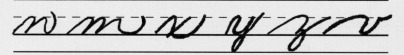

To help students evaluate their writing, ask questions such as these:
Is your **x** crossed in the middle of the slant stroke?
Is your **y** about the same width as the model?

Join letters to *n, m, x, y, z, v.*

Notice how you join each pair of letters.   Write the words.

ni   ni   ni → *ninth*

xc   xc   xc   *except*

mm   mm   *swimming*

ze   ze   ze   *zero*

ym   ym   *enjoyment*

CHECKSTROKE ALERT

Join *v* and *o* at the midline.

Write *volcano,*
not *volcano.*

vo   vo   vo   *volcano*

E V A L U A T E   Circle your best joining. Circle your best word.

21

Ask students to write a paragraph explaining why they think swimming, or any other kind of exercise, is good for them. Participate by describing your favorite form of exercise.

Name _____

Write.

n   n   n   m   m   m

x   x   x   y   y   y

y   y   y   v   v   v

ng   ng   ng   young

yi   yi   yi   trying

zy   zy   zy   lazy

CHECKSTROKE ALERT

ve   ve   ve   inventor

EVALUATE Circle your best letter. Circle your best word.

Copyright © Zaner-Bloser, Inc.   PRACTICE MASTER 7

PRACTICE MASTER 7

Name _____

Write.

me   me   me   women

xc   xc   xc   excuse

ze   ze   ze   dozen

CHECKSTROKE ALERT

vy   vy   vy   heavy

a poor excuse

a dozen eggs

a heavy meal

EVALUATE Circle your best joining. Circle your best word.

PRACTICE MASTER 8   Copyright © Zaner-Bloser, Inc.

PRACTICE MASTER 8

LETTER JOININGS

Draw students' attention to the undercurve endings of **n, m,** and **x.**
Model how to join these letters to

- an undercurve: **nt, me, xi**
- a downcurve: **ng, mo, xa**
- an overcurve: **nn, mm, xy**

Point out that **y** and **z** end with an overcurve.
Model how to join these letters to

- an undercurve: **ye, yi, zi, zl**
- a downcurve: **ya, zo**
- an overcurve: **ym, zz**

Explain that **v** ends with a checkstroke.
Model how to join **v** to

- an undercurve: **vi, ve**
- a downcurve: **va, vo**
- an overcurve: **vy**

(visual, auditory)

CORRECTIVE STRATEGY

vo   **NOT**   *vo*

Be sure to write the checkstroke before joining to **o.**

Practice Masters 86, 87, and 88 provide additional practice.

21

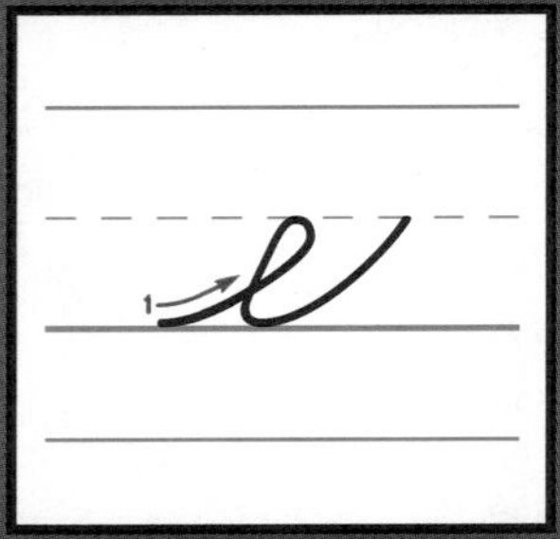

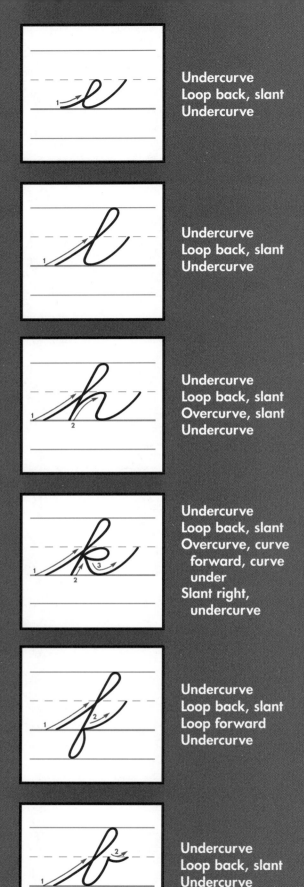

Undercurve
Loop back, slant
Undercurve

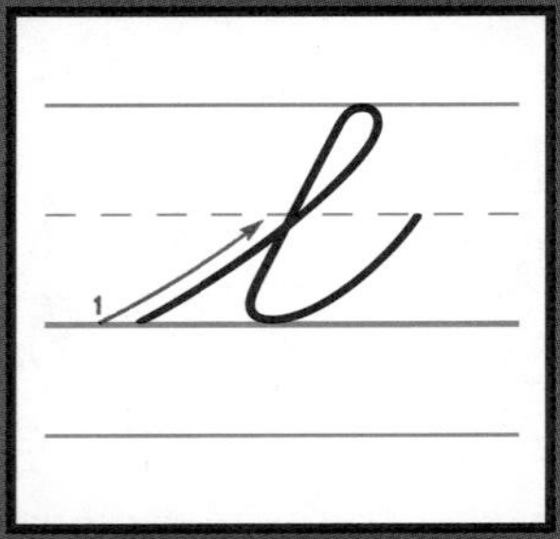

Undercurve
Loop back, slant
Undercurve

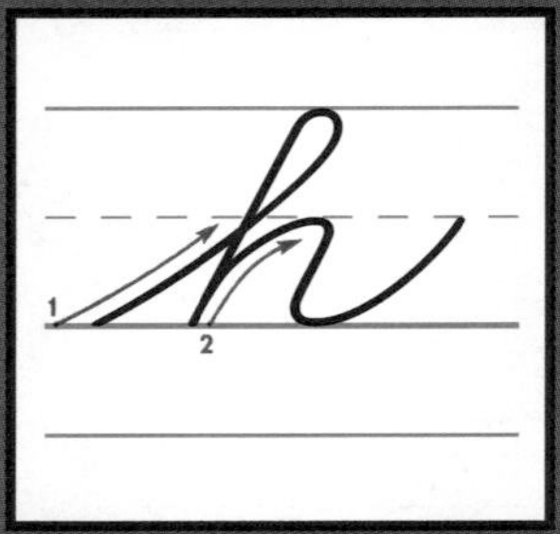

Undercurve
Loop back, slant
Overcurve, slant
Undercurve

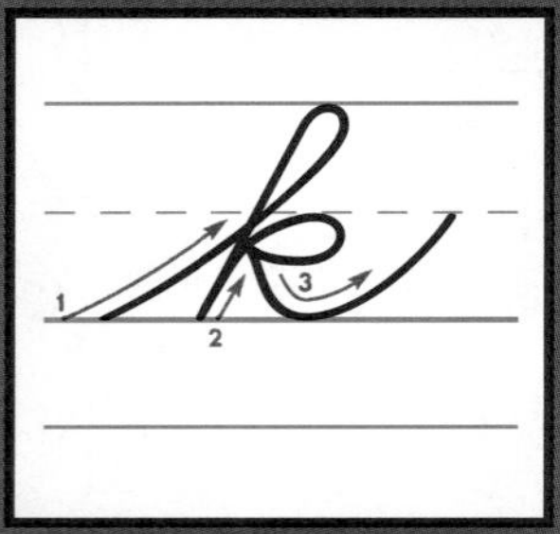

Undercurve
Loop back, slant
Overcurve, curve forward, curve under
Slant right, undercurve

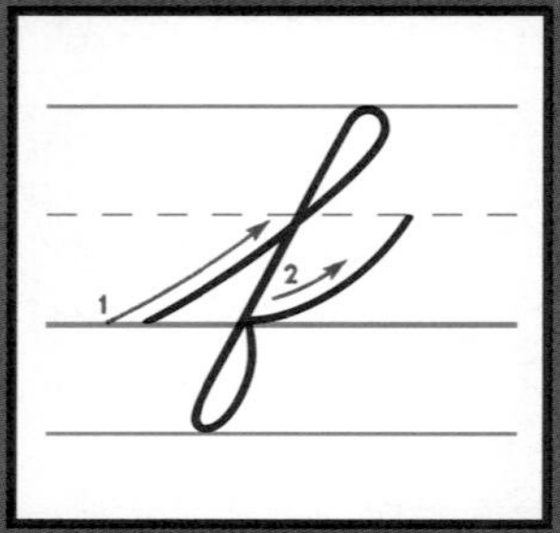

Undercurve
Loop back, slant
Loop forward
Undercurve

Undercurve
Loop back, slant
Undercurve
Checkstroke

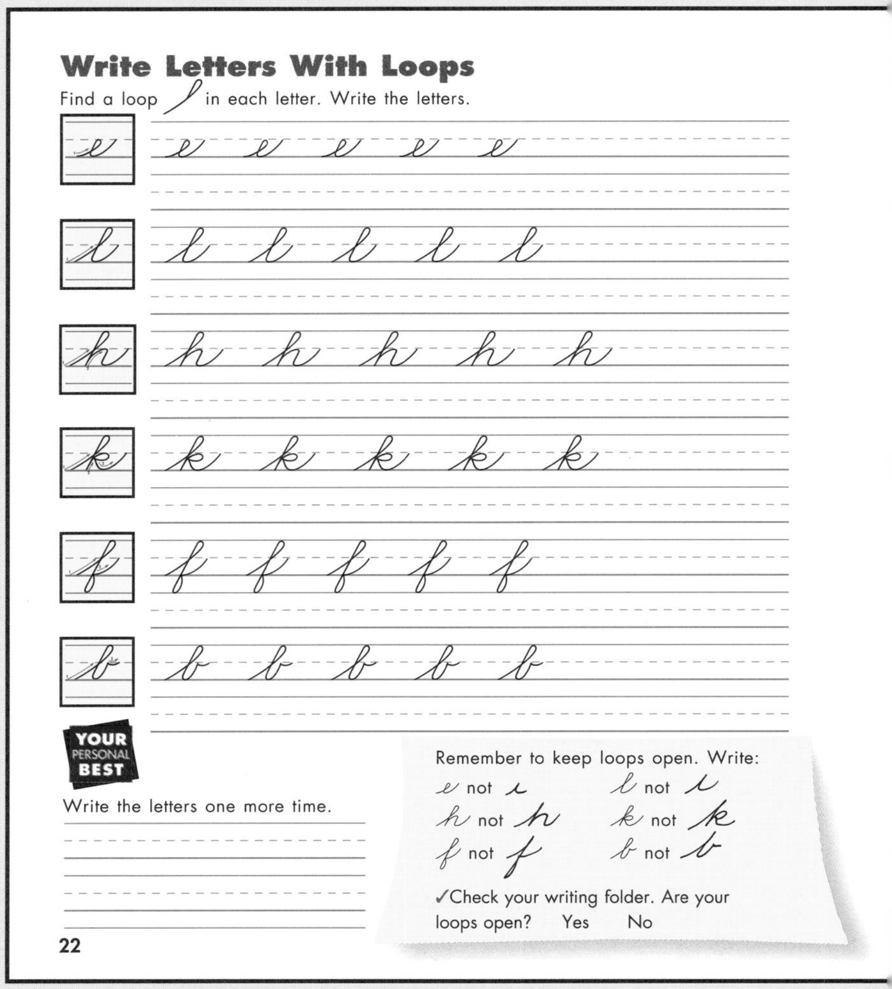

Write Letters With Loops

Find a loop in each letter. Write the letters.

YOUR PERSONAL BEST

Write the letters one more time.

Remember to keep loops open. Write:

e not e, l not l, h not h, k not k, f not f, b not b

✓Check your writing folder. Are your loops open? Yes No

22

Model the Writing

Write **e, l, h, k, f,** and **b** on guidelines as you say the stroke descriptions. To help students visualize the letters, model each letter in the air. Have students echo the stroke descriptions as they form the letters in the air. Ask questions such as these:
Which letters begin and end with an undercurve? *(e, l, h, k, f)*
How does **b** end? *(with a checkstroke)*
(visual, auditory, kinesthetic)

A Closer Look

Have students look at the models of the letters and notice the following: The letters **l, h, k, f,** and **b** have loops that close near the midline. The loop of **e** closes between the midline and the baseline. (visual)

Evaluate

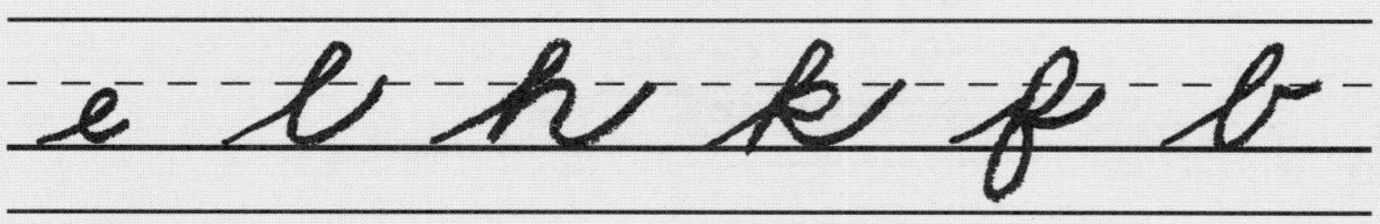

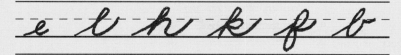

To help students evaluate their writing, ask questions such as these:
Does your **e** touch the midline?
Do your tall letters touch the headline?

Join letters to *e, l, h, k, f, b.*

Notice how you join each pair of letters.

Write the words.

fl fl fl → *flight*

lo lo lo → *loose*

ha ha ha → *happened*

ex ex ex → *exercise*

kn kn kn → *known*

CHECKSTROKE
ALERT

Join *b* and *e* at the midline.

be be be

Write *beautiful,*
not *beautiful.*

beautiful

EVALUATE Circle your best joining. Circle your best word.

23

Ask students to write an anecdote beginning with the sentence *It happened late one night.* Participate by suggesting a second sentence, such as *I had gone to bed early.*

Name _____
Write.
e e e l l l
h h h k k k
f f f b b b
hu hu hu huge
lo lo lo o'clock
em em em emptiness

CHECKSTROKE ALERT
bb bb bb bubble

EVALUATE Circle your best letter. Circle your best word.
Copyright © Zaner-Bloser, Inc. **PRACTICE MASTER 9**

PRACTICE MASTER 9

Name _____
Write.
ki ki ki kitchen
fo fo fo following
en en en written

CHECKSTROKE ALERT
br br br break
a bad break
the kitchen table
the following week

EVALUATE Circle your best joining. Circle your best word.
PRACTICE MASTER 10 Copyright © Zaner-Bloser, Inc.

PRACTICE MASTER 10

LETTER JOININGS

Draw students' attention to the undercurve endings of **e, l, h, k,** and **f.**
Model how to join these letters to

- an undercurve: **et, lu, hi, ks, fr**
- a downcurve: **eq, ld, ho, ka**
- an overcurve: **en, lv, fy**

Explain that **b** ends with a checkstroke.
Model how to join **b** to

- an undercurve: **be, bi, bl, br**
- a downcurve: **ba, bo**
- an overcurve: **by**

(visual, auditory)

CORRECTIVE STRATEGY

lo **NOT** *lo*

Retrace to begin **o.**

Practice Masters 89, 90, and 91 provide additional practice.

23

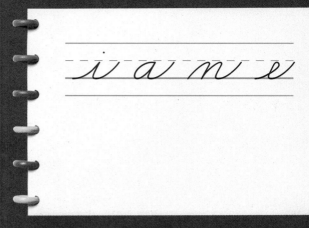

i a m e

Discuss with students how lowercase cursive letters are grouped: undercurve, downcurve, overcurve, letters with loops. Provide opportunities for students to practice the formation of each letter on handwriting guidelines. (visual, auditory, kinesthetic)

COACHING HINT

Use the chalkboard for teaching and practicing the basic strokes, letters, and numerals. Students having difficulty with fine motor skills may benefit from the increased spacing the chalkboard provides. Since erasing is easy, identifying and correcting errors becomes a simpler task. (visual, auditory, kinesthetic)

Practice Master 92 provides an additional review of the lowercase letters.

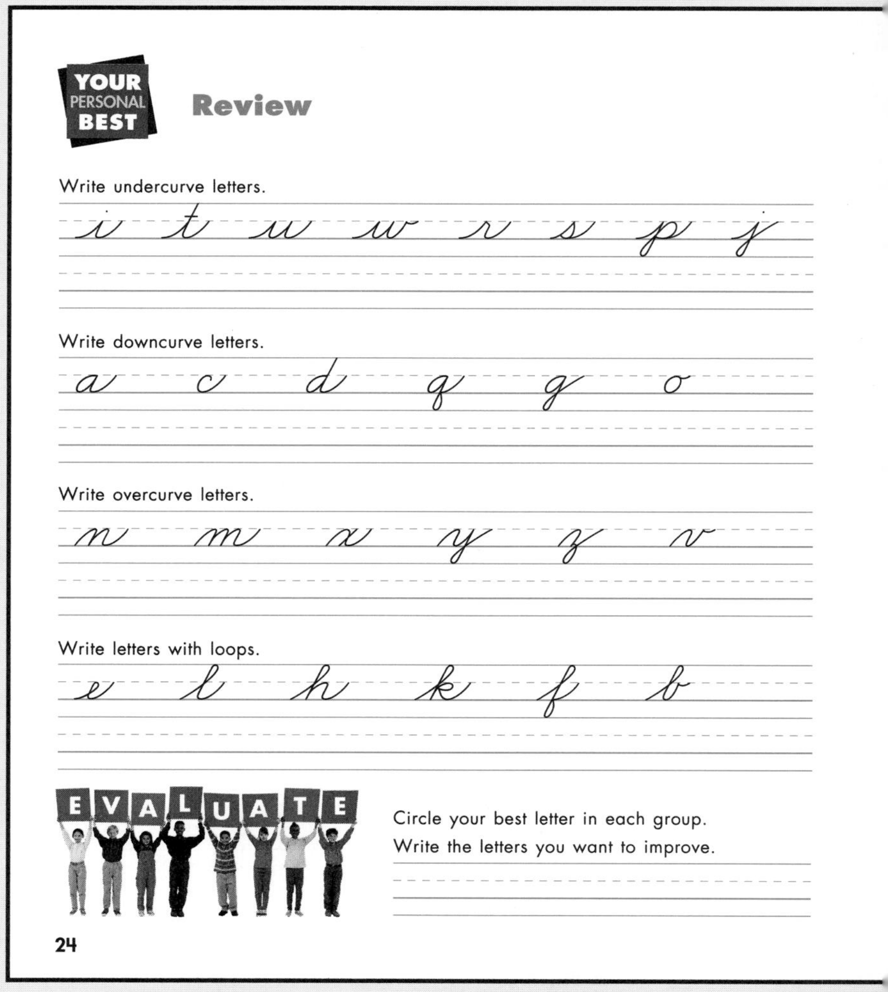

YOUR PERSONAL BEST   **Review**

Write undercurve letters.

i t u w r s p j

Write downcurve letters.

a c d q g o

Write overcurve letters.

n m x y z v

Write letters with loops.

e l h k f b

EVALUATE

Circle your best letter in each group.
Write the letters you want to improve.

24

EVALUATE

Guide students through the self-evaluation process, asking them to focus on the size and shape of each letter. Encourage them to explain why one letter might be better than another. (visual, auditory)

Lowercase *i* and *e* begin with an undercurve . Join letters to an undercurve.

 i   *mi*   *di*   *ji*   *bi*

e   *he*   *se*   *ye*   *we*

Lowercase *o* and *a* begin with a downcurve. Join letters to a downcurve.

 o   *ro*   *fo*   *jo*   *oo*

a   *la*   *ca*   *ga*   *va*

Lowercase *n* and *y* begin with an overcurve. Join letters to an overcurve.

n   *un*   *kn*   *gn*   *on*

y   *ty*   *py*   *zy*   *by*

 EVALUATE

✓Check your writing folder. Do you join lowercase letters correctly?   Yes   No

LETTER JOININGS

Point out that **i** and **e** begin with undercurves. Model joining undercurve beginning letters to

- undercurve ending letters: **mi, di, he, se**
- overcurve ending letters: **ji, ye**
- checkstroke ending letters: **bi, we**

Explain that **o** and **a** begin with downcurves. Model joining downcurve beginning letters to

- undercurve ending letters: **ro, fo, la, ca**
- overcurve ending letters: **jo, ga**
- checkstroke ending letters: **oo, va**

Explain that **n** and **y** begin with overcurves. Model joining overcurve beginning letters to

- undercurve ending letters: **un, kn, ty, py**
- overcurve ending letters: **gn, zy**
- checkstroke ending letters: **on, by**

(visual, auditory)

EVALUATE

Guide students through the self-evaluation process, focusing on joinings. Ask if they joined the checkstroke letters at the midline. (visual, auditory)

Invite students to write jokes or riddles in cursive. Allow students to take turns sharing the jokes or riddles with classmates. Any issue of *Highlights for Children* will provide several riddles students may use as models.

COACHING HINT

As students continue the transition from manuscript to cursive, they may find that maintaining correct spacing between letters is difficult. The joining stroke between letters must be wide enough to allow for good spacing. There should be just enough space for a minimum-sized oval. Suggest students practice joinings to reinforce both fluent strokes and good spacing. (visual, kinesthetic)

Writing Uppercase Letters

Uppercase letters are important for writing names of people, places, and things.

Write some names that begin with an uppercase letter.

In the following pages, you will write uppercase letters that are grouped by common strokes. You will learn when to join an uppercase letter to the letter that follows. You will focus on size and shape to help make your writing legible.

26

UNIT SUMMARY

This page tells students about the content, organization, and focus of the unit. Students are reminded that uppercase letters begin specific names. Then they are introduced to the first two keys to legibility for uppercase letters: size and shape. The lessons that follow emphasize uppercase letter formation and joinings and provide opportunities for writing uppercase letters in different contexts. Evaluations focus on letter size and shape. The Teacher Edition includes information on optional joinings.

PREVIEW THE UNIT

Preview the unit with students, calling attention to these features:

• letter models with numbered directional arrows
• guidelines for student writing directly beneath handwriting models
• hints about joining uppercase letters to the letter that follows
• opportunities to write letters independently after practice
• brief independent writing activities
• opportunities to evaluate letter size and shape

Keys to Legibility: Size and Shape

Uppercase letters are formed from these strokes. Write the strokes.

undercurve	downcurve	overcurve	slant

All uppercase letters are tall letters. Write these tall letters.

A B C D E F G H I

J K L M N O P Q R

S T U V W X Y Z

Write these three letters with descenders.

J Y Z

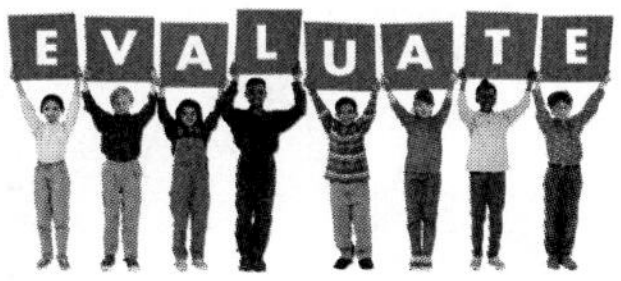

EVALUATE

Compare your letters with the models.
Are they the same size and shape?   Yes   No

27

MODEL THE WRITING

Write the basic strokes on guidelines as you name each stroke. Invite students to say the names as they write the strokes in the air. Point out that uppercase cursive letters are formed from these basic strokes. Then model writing several uppercase letters on the guidelines. Remind students that all uppercase letters are tall letters. Have volunteers name the three uppercase letters that have descenders (**J, Y, Z**). (visual, auditory, kinesthetic)

EVALUATE

Guide students through the self-evaluation process. Then ask them if they can read their letters easily. Encourage them to explain why or why not. (visual, auditory)

Downcurve
Undercurve
Slant, undercurve

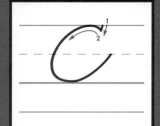

Slant
Downcurve
Undercurve

Slant
Downcurve, loop
Downcurve,
  undercurve

Downcurve
Undercurve
Loop, curve right

COACHING HINT

Students' progress in handwriting is greater when short, intensive periods of instruction are used. Fifteen minutes for a lesson is optimal.

Write Downcurve Letters

Find a downcurve (in each letter. Write the letters and joinings.

a   a   a   a   a   a

C   C   C   C   C   C

E   E   E   E   E   E

O   O   O   O   O   O

JOINING ALERT

a, C, and *E* are joined to the letter that follows.
O is not joined to the letter that follows.

Am   Cl   Ed   Or

YOUR PERSONAL BEST Write the letters one more time.

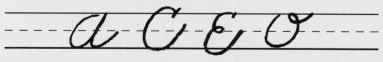

28

MODEL THE WRITING

Write **A, C, E,** and **O** on guidelines as you say the stroke descriptions. To help students visualize the letters, model each letter on the chalkboard. Have students echo the stroke descriptions as they form the letters on their desks. Ask questions such as these:
Which letters end at the midline? *(A, C, E)*
How does **O** end? *(with loop, curve right)*
(visual, auditory, kinesthetic)

A CLOSER LOOK

Have students look at the models of the letters and notice the following: The letters **A** and **O** begin with a downcurve just below the headline; **C** and **E** begin at the headline with slant, downcurve. (visual)

EVALUATE

a   C   E   O

To help students evaluate their writing, ask questions such as these:
Are your letters the right size?
Are your **A** and **O** closed?

Write names of book and movie characters.
Begin each name with an uppercase letter.

Addy   *Aladdin*

Cam   *Charlotte*

Eloise   *Encyclopedia*

Otis   *Oliver*

On Your Own Write the names of your favorite book and movie characters.

EVALUATE

Does each *a* and *O* begin with a downcurve?

Yes No

Does each *C* and *E* begin with a slant?

Yes No

29

LETTER JOININGS

Draw students' attention to the undercurve endings of **A, C,** and **E.** Model how to join these letters to

- an undercurve: **Ar, Cl, Es**
- a downcurve: **Ac, Ca, Ed**
- an overcurve: **Am, Cy, Ex**

Remind students that **O** is not joined to the letter that follows. Model several examples, such as **Ob, Oa,** and **Om.** (visual, auditory)

CORRECTIVE STRATEGY

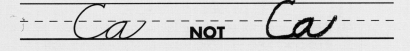

Ca **NOT** *Ca*

The undercurve to downcurve joining becomes a doublecurve. At the end of the doublecurve, you retrace. The retrace ends about halfway between the midline and baseline.

Write Away

Ask students to write a list of questions they would like to ask their favorite book character. Participate by sharing questions you might ask.

I'm glad you asked that question.

Name

Write.

a a a   c c c

E E E   O O O

JOINING ALERT
a, c, and *E* are joined to the letter that follows.
O is not joined to the letter that follows.

Af Af Af   Africa

Cy Cy Cy   Cyprus

Eg Eg Eg   Egypt

On On On   Ontario

EVALUATE Circle your best letter. Circle your best word.

Copyright © Zaner-Bloser, Inc.   **PRACTICE MASTER II**

PRACTICE MASTER II

Name

Write titles of books.

Meet Addy

Charlotte's Web

Eloise

Otis Spofford

Addy Learns a Lesson

Encyclopedia Brown

Oliver Twist

EVALUATE Circle the title you wrote best.

PRACTICE MASTER I2   Copyright © Zaner-Bloser, Inc.

PRACTICE MASTER I2

Practice Masters 93 and 94 provide additional practice.

29

Curve forward,
slant
Overcurve, slant
Undercurve

Curve forward,
slant
Overcurve, slant
Overcurve, slant
Undercurve

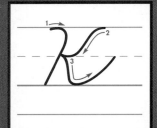

Curve forward,
slant, (lift)
Doublecurve
Curve forward,
undercurve

Curve forward,
slant, (lift)
Curve back, slant
Retrace, loop,
curve right

COACHING HINT

Evaluation of slant can be done by drawing lines through the slant strokes of the letters. The lines should be parallel and should show the correct degree of forward slant. (visual, kinesthetic)

Write Curve Forward Letters

Find a curve forward ⟩ in each letter. Write the letters and joinings.

n	n n n n n
m	m m m m m
K	K K K K K
H	H H H H H

JOINING ALERT

n, m, K, and H are joined to the letter that follows.

Ni Mo Ka Hi

YOUR PERSONAL BEST Write the letters one more time.

30

MODEL THE WRITING

Write **N, M, K,** and **H** on guidelines as you say the stroke descriptions. To help students visualize the letters, model each letter on the palm of your hand. Have students echo the stroke descriptions as they form the letters on the palms of their hands. Ask questions such as these:

How are **H** and **K** alike? *(They have the same beginning strokes and one lift.)*
How does **N** differ from **M**? *(M has one more overcurve, slant.)*
(visual, auditory, kinesthetic)

A CLOSER LOOK

Have students look at the models of the letters and notice the following: There are two slant strokes in **N**, three in **M**, one in **K**, and two in **H**. All slant strokes are parallel. (visual)

EVALUATE

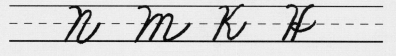

To help students evaluate their writing, ask questions such as these:
Is your **N** about the same width as the model?
Is the second overcurve in your **M** shorter than the first?

Write names of special days.
Begin each important word with an uppercase letter.

National Handwriting Day

Hat Day

Memory Day

Be Kind to Animals Day

Halfway Day

On Your Own Write the name of a special day you like to celebrate.

E V A L U A T E

Do *n, m, k,* and *H*
begin with a curve forward?

Yes   No

Circle your best word.

31

LETTER JOININGS

Draw students' attention to the undercurve endings of **N, M,** and **K.**
Model how to join these letters to

- an undercurve: **Ni, Me, Kl**
- a downcurve: **Na, Mc, Ko**
- an overcurve: **My**

Explain that **H** ends with a curve right.
Model how to join **H** to

- an undercurve: **He, Hi, Hu**
- a downcurve: **Ha, Ho**
- an overcurve: **Hy**

(visual, auditory)

CORRECTIVE STRATEGY

Ha   **NOT**   *Ha*

After closing the loop in **H,** write a doublecurve.

Provide the dates for the special days
listed on page 31.

National Handwriting Day: January 23
Hat Day: January 20
Memory Day: March 1
Be Kind to Animals Day: April 10
Halfway Day: July 2

Ask students to select a day and
describe how they would celebrate it.
Participate by telling how you might
celebrate a special day.

Name

Write

n   n   n   m   m   m

k   k   k   H   H   H

JOINING ALERT
n, m, k, and *H* are joined to the letter that follows.

Ne   Ne   Ne   Nepal

Mo   Mo   Mo   Morocco

Ke   Ke   Ke   Kenya

Ho   Ho   Ho   Holland

EVALUATE Circle your best letter. Circle your best word.

Copyright © Zaner-Bloser, Inc.   **PRACTICE MASTER 13**

PRACTICE MASTER 13

Name

Write names of special days.
National Freedom Day

May Day

World Hello Day

Kids' Day

Left-Handers' Day

National Nothing Day

Ides of March

EVALUATE Circle the name you wrote best.

PRACTICE MASTER 14   Copyright © Zaner-Bloser, Inc.

PRACTICE MASTER 14

*Practice Masters 95 and 96 provide
additional practice.*

Curve forward,
   slant
Undercurve
Slant, undercurve

Curve forward,
   slant
Undercurve
Slant
Loop back,
   overcurve

Curve forward,
   slant
Overcurve, curve
   down
Loop, overcurve

COACHING HINT

The writing rate will increase as students begin to move the writing hand more freely. Have students practice writing letters and words in large size with crayon on folded newsprint to overcome finger motion. (kinesthetic)

Write Curve Forward Letters

Find a curve forward ⌐ in each letter. Write the letters and joinings.

U U U U U

Y Y Y Y Y

Z Z Z Z Z

JOINING ALERT

U, Y, and *Z* are joined to the letter that follows.

Un   Yi   Ze

YOUR PERSONAL BEST — Write the letters one more time.

32

MODEL THE WRITING

Write **U, Y,** and **Z** on guidelines as you say the stroke descriptions. To help students visualize the letters, model each letter on the chalkboard. Have students echo the stroke descriptions as they form the letters on their desks. Ask questions such as these:
How do all the letters begin? *(with curve forward, slant)*
Which letters have descenders? *(Y, Z)*
(visual, auditory, kinesthetic)

A CLOSER LOOK

Have students look at the models of the letters and notice the following: The letters **U** and **Y** touch the headline twice. The letters **Y** and **Z** have a loop that closes at the baseline. (visual)

EVALUATE

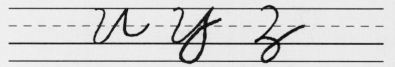

To help students evaluate their writing, ask questions such as these:
Did you pull the slant stroke in your **U** to the baseline?
Does the loop of your **Y** close at the baseline?

Write names of countries.
Begin each name with an uppercase letter.

Uganda   Yemen

New Zealand   Zimbabwe

Uruguay   Zambia

United Kingdom

United States

On Your Own Write the name of a country you would

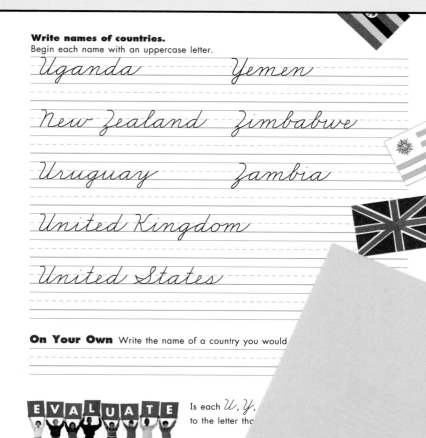

EVALUATE   Is each *U*, *Y*,
to the letter th

Circle your

Ask students to use an encyclopedia to explore another country. Have them write five interesting facts about the country. Participate by naming a country you would like to investigate.

LETTER
Draw students' attention to the
Model how to join **U** to

- an undercu
- a downcu
- an overc

Point out that **Y** and **Z** en
Model how to join these

- an u
- a d
- a

(visual, auditory)

GY

Close the   g **e**.

Name

Write.

U   U   U   Y   Y   Y

Y   Y   Y

JOINING ALERT
U, *Y*, and *Y* are joined to the letter that follows.

Uk   Uk   Uk   Ukraine

Ya   Ya   Ya   Yalta

Zu   Zu   Zu   Zurich

Yu   Yu   Yu   Yucatan

EVALUATE Circle your best letter. Circle your best word.

Copyright © Zaner-Bloser, Inc.   PRACTICE MASTER 15

PRACTICE MASTER 15

Name

Write names of rivers and continents.

Yellowstone (North America)

Uruguay (South America)

Zambezi (Africa)

Yalu (Asia)

Yukon (North America)

Ural (Europe)

Yangtze (Asia)

EVALUATE Circle the name you wrote best.

PRACTICE MASTER 16   Copyright © Zaner-Bloser, Inc.

PRACTICE MASTER 16

Practice Masters 97 and 98 provide additional practice.

33

Curve forward,
   slant
Undercurve
Overcurve

Curve forward,
   slant,
   undercurve (lift)
Slant

Curve forward,
   slant
Undercurve, slant
Undercurve
Overcurve

Write Curve Forward Letters
Find a curve forward ⁊ in each letter. Write the letters and joinings.

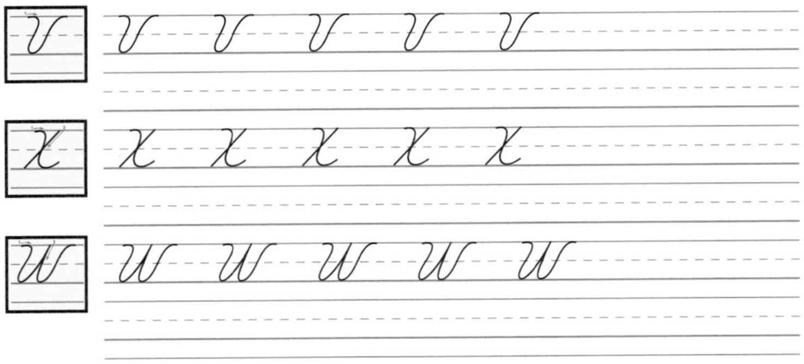

𝒱 𝒱 𝒱 𝒱 𝒱 𝒱

𝒳 𝒳 𝒳 𝒳 𝒳 𝒳

𝒲 𝒲 𝒲 𝒲 𝒲 𝒲

JOINING ALERT

𝒱, 𝒳, and 𝒲 are not joined to the letter that follows.

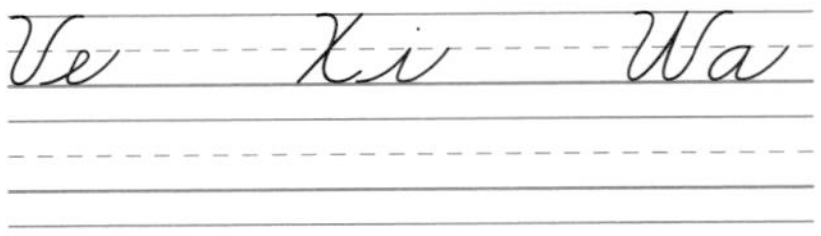

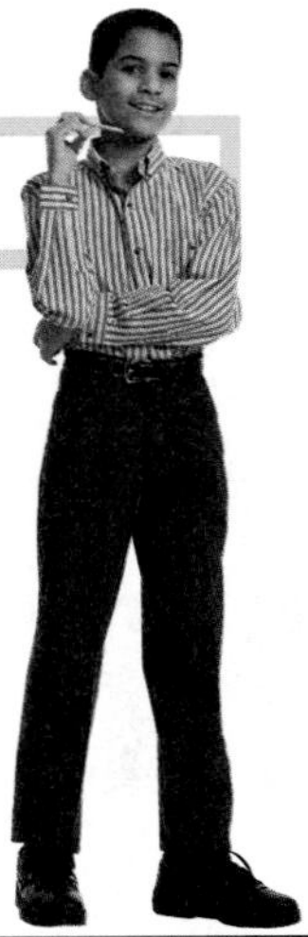

𝒱e   𝒳i   𝒲a

YOUR PERSONAL BEST   Write the letters one more time.

MODEL THE WRITING
Write **V**, **X**, and **W** on guidelines as you say the stroke descriptions. To help students visualize the letters, model each letter on the palm of your hand. Have students echo the stroke descriptions as they form the letters on the palms of their hands. Ask questions such as these:
How are **V** and **W** alike? *(They begin with curve forward, slant, undercurve; they end with an overcurve.)*
Where is the lift in **X**? *(after the undercurve)*
(visual, auditory, kinesthetic)

A CLOSER LOOK
Have students look at the models of the letters and notice the following: Each letter begins just below the headline. The letter **W** touches the headline three times. (visual)

EVALUATE

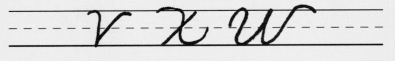

To help students evaluate their writing, ask questions such as these:
Is your **V** about the same width as the model?
Does your **W** begin just below the headline?

Write names of people.
Begin each name with an uppercase letter.

Vera   Vivienne   Varice

Victor   Vincent   Vidor

Washi   Winona   Wilma

Waldo   William   Witt

Xanthe   Xiang   Xena

On Your Own Write a name you like.

EVALUATE   Are your curve forward strokes
smooth and rounded?
                    Yes   No
Circle your best word.

Washi - eagle   Waldo - strong

35

LETTER JOININGS
Remind students that **V** and **W** are not joined to the letter that follows.
Joining **X** is optional. Model several examples, such as **Vi, Xa, Wy**.
(visual, auditory)

CORRECTIVE STRATEGIES

V   **NOT**   *V*

End **V** with an overcurve.

W   **NOT**   *W*

The first undercurve ends at the headline.

Write Away

Ask students to select one of the names
on page 35 and to write a biography
about a real or an imaginary person
with that name. Participate by describing the life of a person of your choice.

Name _____
Write. _____

V   V   V   X   X   X

W   W   W

JOINING ALERT
V, X, and *W* are not joined to the letter that follows.

Ve Ve Ve   Venice

Xo Xo Xo   Xochimilco

Wi Wi Wi   Winnipeg

Wa Wa Wa   Warsaw

EVALUATE Circle your best letter. Circle your best word.

Copyright © Zaner-Bloser, Inc.   **PRACTICE MASTER 17**

PRACTICE MASTER 17

Name _____

Write family names.

Vaccaro	*Waldbaum*
Xanders	*Valentino*
Wong	*Xilas*
Varga	*Washington*
Xing	*Vanderbilt*
Winters	*Xenatos*
Vaughn	*Walker*

EVALUATE Circle the name you wrote best.

PRACTICE MASTER 18   Copyright © Zaner-Bloser, Inc.

PRACTICE MASTER 18

*Practice Masters 98 and 99 provide
additional practice.*

Slant, curve for-
ward and right,
(lift)
Doublecurve,
curve up
Retrace, curve right

Slant, curve for-
ward and right,
(lift)
Doublecurve,
curve up
Retrace, curve
right, (lift)
Slide right

COACHING HINT

Right-handed teachers will better understand
the stroke, visual perspective, and posture of
the left-handed student if they practice the
left-handed position themselves.

Write Doublecurve Letters

Find a doublecurve ∫ in each letter. Write the letters, joinings, and words.

T   T   T   T   T

F   F   F   F   F

JOINING ALERT

T and *F* are not joined to the letter that follows.

Tr   Fa

Troy   Fatima

YOUR PERSONAL BEST Write the letters one more time.

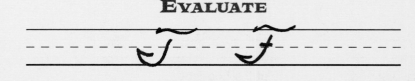

MODEL THE WRITING

Write **T** and **F** on guidelines as you say the stroke descriptions. To
help students visualize the letters, model each letter in the air. Have
students echo the stroke descriptions as they form the letters in the air.
Ask questions such as these:
How does **F** differ from **T**? *(F has a slide right stroke.)*
How many lifts are in **F**? *(two)*
(visual, auditory, kinesthetic)

A CLOSER LOOK

Have students look at the models of the letters and notice the following: Both letters rest on the baseline. The **F** is crossed at the midline.

EVALUATE

T   F

To help students evaluate their writing, ask questions such as these:
Does the doublecurve in your **T** touch the top of the letter?
Does the curve up stroke in your **F** end at the midline?

Write names of United States presidents.
Begin each name with an uppercase letter.

Thomas Jefferson

Millard Fillmore

Theodore Roosevelt

Harry S Truman

John Fitzgerald Kennedy

On Your Own Write the name of the person who is president now.

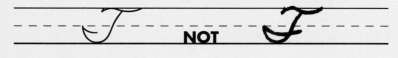

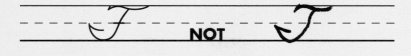

EVALUATE   Does each T and F have a doublecurve?   Yes   No

Circle the name you wrote best.

37

LETTER JOININGS

Joining **T** and **F** to the letter that follows is optional. Model several examples, such as **Th, Ta, Fo**, and **Fy**. (visual, auditory)

CORRECTIVE STRATEGIES

T   NOT   T

Leave space between curve right and doublecurve strokes.

F   NOT   F

Do not forget to add the slide right stroke.

Ask students to write a paragraph telling why they would or would not like to be president of the United States.

Name _____

Write.

T   T   T   T   T   T

F   F   F   F   F   F

JOINING ALERT
T and F are not joined to the letter that follows.

Tu   Tu   Tu   Turkey

Ti   Ti   Ti   Tijuana

Fr   Fr   Fr   France

Fl   Fl   Fl   Florence

EVALUATE Circle your best letter. Circle your best word.

Copyright © Zaner-Bloser, Inc.   PRACTICE MASTER 19

PRACTICE MASTER 19

Name _____

Write names of First Ladies of the United States.

Julia Tyler

Margaret Taylor

Mary Todd Lincoln

Frances Cleveland

Helen Taft

Florence Harding

Betty Ford

EVALUATE Circle the name you wrote best.

PRACTICE MASTER 20   Copyright © Zaner-Bloser, Inc.

PRACTICE MASTER 20

Practice Master 100 provides additional practice.

Overcurve
Curve down and
   up
Retrace, curve right

Overcurve
Slant
Loop back, over-
   curve

Curve back,
   overcurve
Curve down,
   retrace
Curve forward,
   curve under

COACHING HINT

Correct paper placement is a critical factor in legibility. Check this periodically with each student. (visual)

Write Overcurve Letters

Find an overcurve (in each letter. Write the letters and joinings.

JOINING ALERT

J is joined to the letter that follows.

I and *Q* are not joined to the letter that follows.

Ir   Jo   Qu

YOUR PERSONAL BEST Write the letters one more time.

38

MODEL THE WRITING

Write **I**, **J**, and **Q** on guidelines as you say the stroke descriptions. To help students visualize the letters, model each letter on the chalkboard. Have students echo the stroke descriptions as they form the letters on their desks. Ask questions such as these:
Where do **I** and **J** begin? *(just below the baseline)*
How does **Q** begin? *(with curve back, overcurve)*
(visual, auditory, kinesthetic)

A CLOSER LOOK

Have students look at the models of the letters and notice the following: The letter **I** ends below the midline; **J** ends at the midline; **Q** ends below the baseline. (visual)

EVALUATE

To help students evaluate their writing, ask questions such as these:
Are your letters the correct size?
Do the loops of your **J** close at the baseline?

Write book titles and authors' last names.
Begin important words in each title with an uppercase letter.
Begin each author's name with an uppercase letter.

Isabelle the Itch (Greene)

Anno's Journey (Anno)

Quentin Corn (Stolz)

Like Jake and Me (Jukes)

Journey Home (Uchida)

On Your Own Write the title of one of your favorite books.

EVALUATE

Does each ℐ begin just below the baseline?

Yes   No

Does each ℐ end with an overcurve?

Yes   No

39

LETTER JOININGS

Remind students that **Q** is not joined to the letter that follows. Joining **I** is optional. Model several examples, such as **Ir, Id,** and **Qu.**

Draw students' attention to the overcurve ending of **J.**
Model how to join **J** to

- an undercurve: **Je, Ji**
- a downcurve: **Ja, Jo**

(visual, auditory)

CORRECTIVE STRATEGY

ℐ   **NOT**   *ℐ*

Pause after the curve at the midline, retrace, and curve right.

Ask students to write a paragraph recommending their favorite book to a friend. Participate by sharing your personal recommendation with students.

Name

Write.

ℐ ℐ ℐ   ℐ ℐ ℐ

𝒬 𝒬 𝒬

JOINING ALERT
ℐ is joined to the letter that follows.
ℐ and 𝒬 are not joined to the letter that follows.

Ja Ja Ja   Java

In In In   India

Qu Qu Qu   Quebec

Is Is Is   Israel

EVALUATE Circle your best letter. Circle your best word.

Copyright © Zaner-Bloser, Inc.   PRACTICE MASTER 21

PRACTICE MASTER 21

Name

Write titles of poems and names of poets.
"Jabberwocky" (Carroll)

"I Am Rose" (Stein)

"The Question" (Kuskin)

"January" (Updike)

"I'm Nobody" (Dickinson)

"Queenie" (Jacobs)

"Jonathan Bing" (Brown)

EVALUATE Circle the title you wrote best.

PRACTICE MASTER 22   Copyright © Zaner-Bloser, Inc.

PRACTICE MASTER 22

Practice Masters 101 and 102 provide additional practice.

Undercurve, loop,
  curve forward
Doublecurve,
  curve up
Retrace, curve right

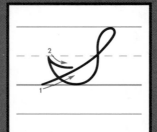

Undercurve, loop
Curve down and
  up
Retrace, curve right

Undercurve
Loop, curve down
Loop, curve under

Doublecurve
Loop, curve down
  and up
Loop, curve right

COACHING HINT

Correct body position influences smoothness. Encourage students to sit comfortably erect with their feet flat on the floor and their hips touching the back of the chair. Both arms rest on the desk. The elbows are off the desk. (kinesthetic)

Write Letters With Loops

Find a loop in each letter. Write the letters and joinings.

JOINING ALERT

G, S, L, and D are not joined to the letter that follows.

Ge   Si   Lo   Dr

YOUR PERSONAL BEST   Write the letters one more time.

40

MODEL THE WRITING

Write **G, S, L,** and **D** on guidelines as you say the stroke descriptions. To help students visualize the letters, model each letter on the palm of your hand. Have students echo the stroke descriptions as they form the letters on the palms of their hands. Ask questions such as these:
Which letters do not begin at the baseline? *(L, D)*
Which letter ends at the headline? *(D)*
(visual, auditory, kinesthetic)

A CLOSER LOOK

Have students look at the models of the letters and notice the following: The loop of **G** and the top loop of **S** and **L** close at the midline. The second loop of **L** and the first loop of **D** rest on the baseline. (visual)

EVALUATE

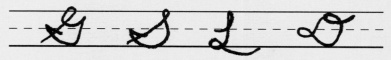

To help students evaluate their writing, ask questions such as these:
Do your letters have correct slant?
Does your **D** touch the baseline twice?

Write silly sentences.
Begin each sentence with an uppercase letter.

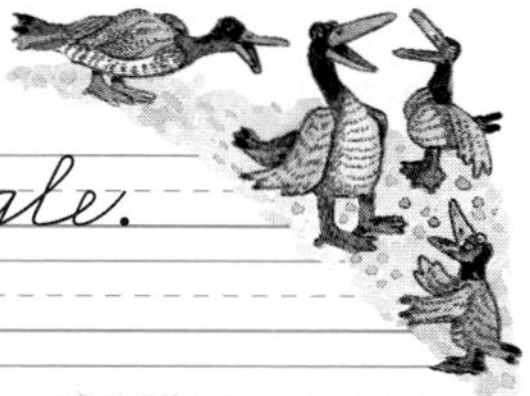

Gaggles of geese giggle.

Sharks sing sea songs.

Look at lizards leaping!

Do deer dine daily?

Little llamas laugh.

On Your Own Write a silly sentence of your own.

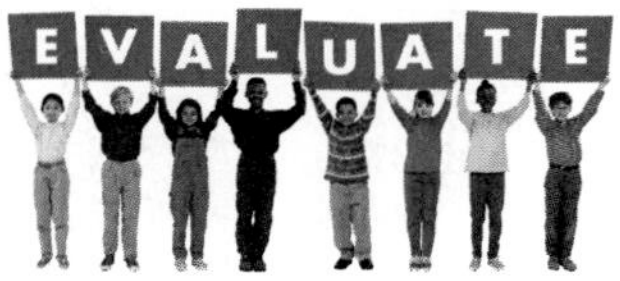

EVALUATE Did you keep your loops open? Yes No

Put a check next to your best sentence.

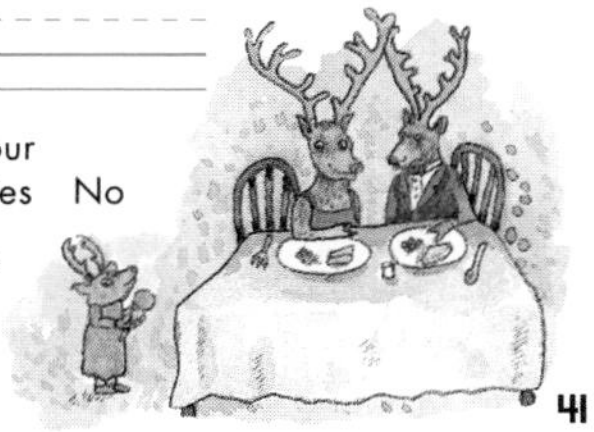

41

LETTER JOININGS

Remind students that **L** and **D** are not joined to the letter that follows. Joining **G** and **S** is optional. Model several examples, such as **Gl, Li, So,** and **Dy**. (visual, auditory)

CORRECTIVE STRATEGIES

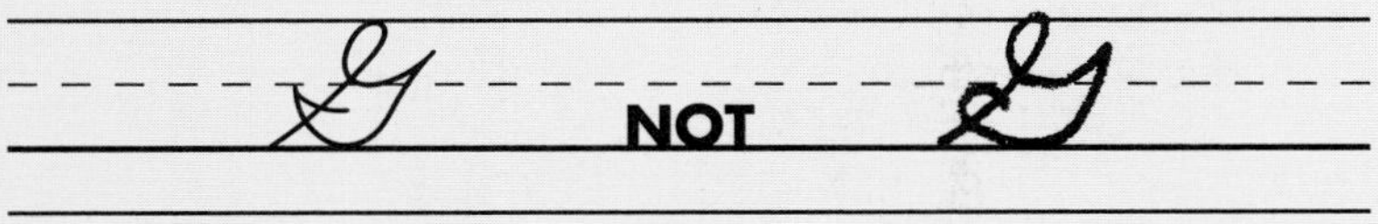

$\mathcal{G}$ NOT $\mathcal{G}$

Pause before the retrace.

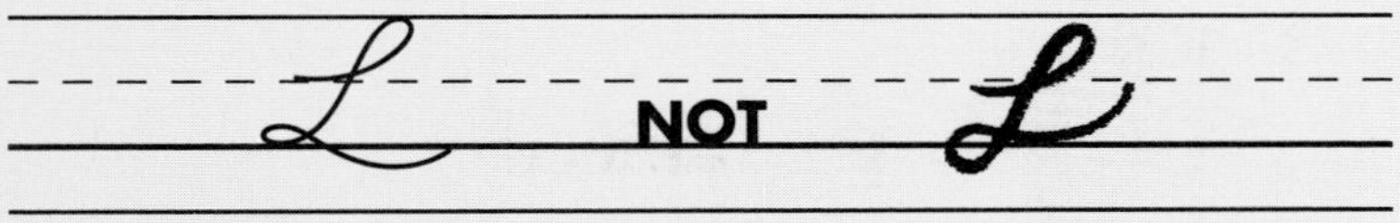

$\mathcal{L}$ NOT $\mathcal{L}$

The ending stroke stops below the baseline.

Write Away

Ask students to write silly sentences with rhyming words. Participate by sharing several rhyming sentences with students.

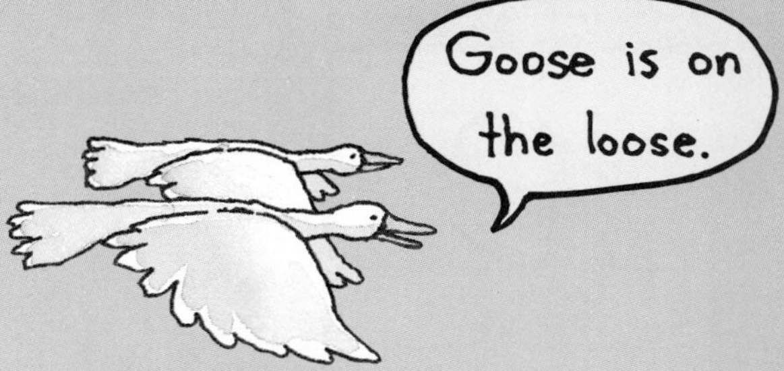

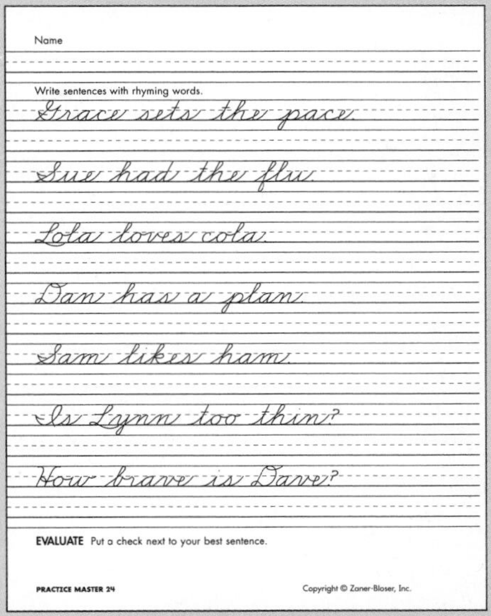

Goose is on the loose.

PRACTICE MASTER 23

PRACTICE MASTER 24

Practice Masters 102, 103, and 104 provide additional practice.

Undercurve, slant
Retrace, curve for-
ward and back

Undercurve, slant
Retrace, curve for-
ward and back
Curve forward,
undercurve

Undercurve, slant
Retrace, curve for-
ward, loop
Curve forward and
back
Retrace, curve right

COACHING HINT

Students who have mastered the skill of writing the uppercase and lowercase letters
without models should be given writing
activities that will challenge them and
require thinking.

Write Undercurve-Slant Letters

Find an undercurve-slant stroke $\mathcal{1}$ in each letter. Write the letters and joinings.

$\mathcal{P}$ $\mathcal{P}$ $\mathcal{P}$ $\mathcal{P}$ $\mathcal{P}$ $\mathcal{P}$

$\mathcal{R}$ $\mathcal{R}$ $\mathcal{R}$ $\mathcal{R}$ $\mathcal{R}$ $\mathcal{R}$

$\mathcal{B}$ $\mathcal{B}$ $\mathcal{B}$ $\mathcal{B}$ $\mathcal{B}$ $\mathcal{B}$

JOINING ALERT

$\mathcal{R}$ is joined to the letter that follows.
$\mathcal{P}$ and $\mathcal{B}$ are not joined to the letter that follows.

Pa   Re   Br

YOUR PERSONAL BEST   Write the letters one more time.

42

MODEL THE WRITING

Write **P, R,** and **B** on guidelines as you say the stroke descriptions. To
help students visualize the letters, model each letter on the chalkboard. Have students echo the stroke descriptions as they form the
letters on their desks. Ask questions such as these:
Where does each letter begin? *(at the midline)*
Which letters have a retrace? *(all)*
(visual, auditory, kinesthetic)

A CLOSER LOOK

Have students look at the models of the letters and notice the following: The letters **P** and **R** curve forward and back to the slant stroke; **B**
curves forward and loops. The ending stroke of **B** touches the slant
stroke. *(visual)*

EVALUATE

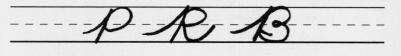

To help students evaluate their writing, ask questions such as these:
Do your **P, R,** and **B** begin at the midline?
Are the forward curves of your **B** parallel with the slant stroke?

Write names of state capitals.
Begin each name with an uppercase letter.

Providence, Rhode Island

Baton Rouge, Louisiana

Phoenix, Arizona

Boise, Idaho

Raleigh, North Carolina

On Your Own Write the name of your state capital.

E V A L U A T E

Does each *P*, *R*, and *B* begin at the midline? Yes No
Circle your best letters.

43

Write Away

Ask students to write and illustrate a travel brochure for one of the places on page 43. Participate by describing a place of your choice.

PROVIDENCE IS FABULOUS

LETTER JOININGS

Remind students that **P** is not joined to the letter that follows. Joining **B** is optional. Model several examples, such as **Pl, Pa, Bo,** and **By.**

Draw students' attention to the undercurve ending of **R.**
Model how to join **R** to
- an undercurve: **Re, Ri**
- a downcurve: **Ra, Ro**
- an overcurve: **Ry**

(visual, auditory)

CORRECTIVE STRATEGY

Ra **NOT** *Ra*

Uppercase **R** is joined to the letter that follows.

Name

Write.
P P P R R R

B B B

JOINING ALERT
R is joined to the letter that follows.
P and *B* are not joined to the letter that follows.

Ru Ru Ru Russia

Po Po Po Portugal

Ba Ba Ba Barbados

Pa Pa Pa Paraguay

EVALUATE Circle your best letter. Circle your best word.

Copyright © Zaner-Bloser, Inc.   **PRACTICE MASTER 25**

PRACTICE MASTER 25

Name

Write names of world capitals.
Panama City, Panama

Lisbon, Portugal

Reykjavik, Iceland

Moscow, Russia

Bucharest, Romania

Brussels, Belgium

Brasilia, Brazil

EVALUATE Circle the name you wrote best.

PRACTICE MASTER 26   Copyright © Zaner-Bloser, Inc.

PRACTICE MASTER 26

Practice Masters 104 and 105 provide additional practice.

KEYS TO LEGIBILITY: SIZE AND SHAPE

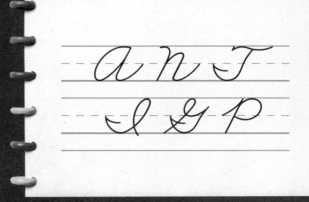

Discuss with students how uppercase cursive letters are grouped: downcurve, curve forward, doublecurve, overcurve, letters with loops, undercurve-slant. Provide opportunities for students to practice the formation of each letter on handwriting guidelines. (visual, auditory, kinesthetic)

Practice Master 106 provides an additional review of the uppercase letters.

YOUR PERSONAL BEST   Review

Write downcurve letters.

A   C   E   O

Write curve forward letters.

N   M   K   H   U   Y   Z   V   X   W

Write doublecurve letters.

T   F

Write overcurve letters.

I   J   Q

Write letters with loops.

G   S   L   D

Write undercurve-slant letters.

P   R   B

EVALUATE

Circle your best letter in each group.
Write the letters you want to improve.

44

EVALUATE

Guide students through the self-evaluation process, asking them to focus on the size and shape of each letter. Encourage them to explain why one letter might be better than another. (visual, auditory)

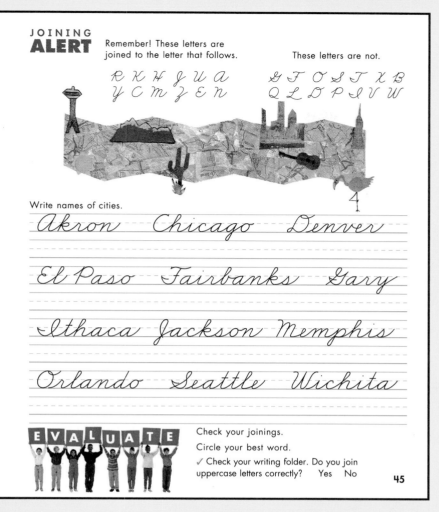

JOINING ALERT

Remember! These letters are joined to the letter that follows.

These letters are not.

R K H J U A Y C M Z E N

G F O S T X B Q L D P I V W

Write names of cities.

Akron   Chicago   Denver

El Paso   Fairbanks   Gary

Ithaca   Jackson   Memphis

Orlando   Seattle   Wichita

EVALUATE

Check your joinings.

Circle your best word.

✓ Check your writing folder. Do you join uppercase letters correctly?   Yes   No

45

EVALUATE

Guide students through the self-evaluation process, focusing on joinings. Encourage them to explain why one joining or word might be better than another. (visual, auditory)

Certificates of Progress should be awarded to those students who show notable handwriting progress and Certificates of Excellence to those who progress to the top levels of handwriting proficiency.

Write Away

Ask students to use an almanac to research the cities named on page 45 and to write a statement about each one; for example, *In Orlando, Florida, you'll find several amusement parks.* (visual, kinesthetic)

COACHING HINT

Demonstrate the technique of drawing a horizontal line with a ruler along the tops of letters to show proper size. Have students practice this technique periodically to evaluate their letter size in curriculum areas that require handwriting, especially those that involve the writing of sentences or paragraphs. Students who have difficulty with proper size of letters should write on paper with a midline and descender space. (visual, auditory, kinesthetic)

Writing for Yourself

Sometimes you write just for yourself. For example, your list of each day's homework assignments is usually for your eyes only.

What else do you write just for yourself?

_____

_____

_____

_____

When you write for yourself, you don't have to be as neat as when you write for someone else. But your writing must still be legible. You should be able to read what you have written now and at some future time, too.

In the following pages, you will write lists, address-book entries, and a schedule for yourself. You will write smaller on notebook paper that does not have a midline, and you will focus on the size and shape of your letters to help make your writing legible.

46

UNIT SUMMARY

This unit is the first of three units that link audience and legibility. This page tells students about the content, organization, and focus of the unit. Then students are introduced to smaller writing on new guidelines. The lessons that follow have writing activities in which students write for themselves. Evaluations focus on smaller letter size and shape. The primary goal for students is to be able to read their own writing.

PREVIEW THE UNIT

Preview the unit with students, calling attention to these features:

- new guidelines without a midline and a descender space
- samples of writing to evaluate
- hints about forming legible letters
- independent writing activities
- opportunities to evaluate letter size and shape and legibility
- a writing activity for manuscript maintenance

Keys to Legibility: Size and Shape

Now that you know how to form each letter, you can write smaller and faster. Here are some things to remember so that your writing will still be legible.

Your tall letters should not touch the headline.

t T h H l L b B k K

Write some tall letters.

_____

_____

Your short letters should be half the size of your tall letters.

a c e i m n o r x u

Write some short letters.

_____

_____

Your descenders should not go too far below the baseline.

f g j f p q y y z z

Write the letters with descenders.

_____

_____

Did you write in the new size?	Yes	No
Are all your tall letters the same size?	Yes	No
Are all your short letters the same size?	Yes	No

47

MODEL THE WRITING

Model writing a tall letter, a short letter, and a letter with a descender, noting the placement of each letter on the new guidelines. Remind students that all letters of the same size should be the same height. (visual, auditory, kinesthetic)

EVALUATE

Guide students through the self-evaluation process. Then ask them if they can read their letters easily. Encourage them to explain why or why not. (visual, auditory)

WRITING FOR YOURSELF

To provide more opportunities to write for themselves, you may wish to ask students to consider legibility as they write:

- **journal entries**
- **writing webs and other graphic organizers**
- **recipes**
- **street directions**

bag

Before students begin, remind them to adjust their writing to the new handwriting lines. Help them group the letters according to size, and provide opportunities to practice proper placement of each letter on the hand-writing lines.

- Tall letters should not touch the headline. Lowercase **b, d, f, h, k, l,** and **t** are tall. All uppercase letters are tall.

- Short letters are half the size of tall letters. Lowercase **a, c, e, g, i, j, m, n, o, p, q, r, s, u, v, w, x, y,** and **z** are short.

- Letters with descenders extend below the baseline. Lowercase **f, g, j, p, q, y,** and **z** have descenders. Uppercase **J, Y,** and **Z** have descenders.

(visual, auditory, kinesthetic)

48

Write Lists

Sometimes you write lists to keep track of things.

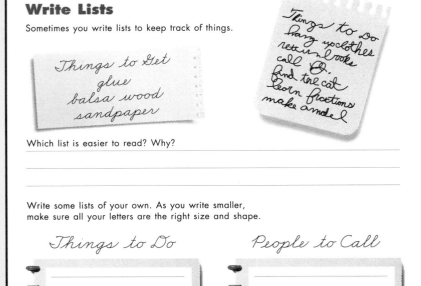

Which list is easier to read? Why?

_____

_____

Write some lists of your own. As you write smaller, make sure all your letters are the right size and shape.

Things to Do   **People to Call**

E V A L U A T E   Did you write smaller?   Yes   No

Are your short letters half the size
of your tall letters?   Yes   No

48

EVALUATE

After students have evaluated the size and shape of their letters, ask if their writing is legible. Ask them to explain why or why not. (visual, auditory)

On Your Own

Some people keep lists for fun. You might start a list now that you add to for the rest of your life! Here are some ideas of things to keep track of. Check one to try this week, and begin your list below.

☐ license plates   ☐ baseball cards   ☐ foreign cars
☐ books   ☐ funny signs   ☐ new words
☐ birds   ☐ places   ☐ other

EVALUATE

Can you read your list easily?   Yes   No
Will you be able to read it later?   Yes   No

Write Away

Ask students to "take inventory" and write a list of things in their desks. Participate by naming several things in your desk.

COACHING HINT

Draw the new writing lines on one side of 9" by 12" pieces of oaktag, and laminate one piece for each student. Students can use these as "slates" by practicing their smaller handwriting with a wipe-off crayon. The reverse side can be used for such things as letter activities. (visual, kinesthetic)

Practice Masters 69–76 are available for use with this unit.

EVALUATE

Have students determine whether their writing is legible in the new size. Ask them to look first at their tall letters, next at their short letters, and then at their letters with descenders. Suggest students choose one group of letters, such as tall letters, and write several rows of letters of that group. (visual, auditory, kinesthetic)

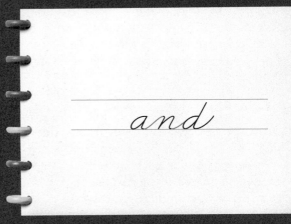

and

Before students begin, remind them to adjust their writing to the new handwriting lines. Emphasize correct joinings by highlighting the joining strokes in words students write on the chalkboard. It may be helpful to review joinings of uppercase letters by creating a simple chart to show letters that join, letters that do not join, and letters that may or may not join. (visual, auditory, kinesthetic)

JOIN
A, C, E, N, M, K,
H, U, Y, Z, J, R

DO NOT JOIN
O, V, W, Q, L, D, P

OPTIONAL
X, T, F, I, G, S, B

Keep an Address Book

Sometimes you write addresses and phone numbers in a book.

To update the page, cross out the entry for Sharon.

Write a new entry.
Sharon Ives
32 Lark Lane
Ames, Iowa
50010
(515)555-7666

Complete the entry for Bob. Write his phone number.
(419)555-1718

Name	*Sharon Ives*
Address	*71 Beach Road*
	Lehi, Utah 84043
Phone	*(801)555-1134*
Name	
Address	
Phone	
Name	*Bob Jordan*
Address	*41 North Avenue*
	Lima, Ohio 45802
Phone	

LEGIBLE LETTERS Remember! Numerals are the size of tall letters.

Are all your tall letters and numerals the same size?   Yes   No
Are your short letters half the size of your tall letters?   Yes   No

EVALUATE

After students have evaluated the size and shape of their letters and numerals, ask if they are able to read their entries. Ask them to explain why or why not. (visual, auditory)

Make an address book. Fill out cards for people you know. Punch a hole in each card, arrange the cards in alphabetical order, and string them together.

Fill out the first card. Then write one of your own.

Name:

Address:

Phone Number:

Birthday:

Other Information:

EVALUATE

Are your numerals tall?	Yes No
Can you read each entry easily?	Yes No

EVALUATE

Have students determine whether writing smaller has affected the shape of their letters. Suggest they choose a word to improve and practice letters and joinings in that word. (visual, auditory, kinesthetic)

Write Away

Ask students to choose one person from their address books to whom they would like to write. Invite them to write a note or letter to that person and to address an envelope.

Karen Smith
377 York Avenue
Houston, Texas 77000

COACHING HINT

Holding the pencil too tightly is a common problem that causes students to tire easily when writing. To overcome this problem, have students crumple a piece of a paper, place it in the palm of the writing hand, and pick up the pencil. This will serve as a reminder not to "squeeze" the pencil. (kinesthetic)

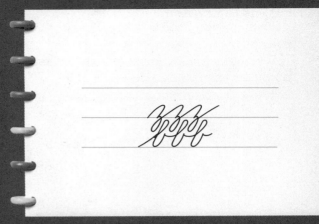

Before students begin, remind them to adjust their writing to the new handwriting lines and to shift words with ascenders so that ascenders of tall letters do not collide with descenders above them. Provide practice in writing tall letters beneath letters with descenders. (visual, auditory, kinesthetic)

Make a Schedule

Sometimes you make a schedule to remind yourself of things you have to do and places you have to be.

Monday	*dentist at 4:00*
	bowling party at 6:00
Tuesday	*piano lesson at 3:00*
Wednesday	

What makes the items in this schedule legible? Check the true statements.

☐ The tall letters are all the same size.

☐ The numerals are the size of tall letters.

☐ The short letters are half the size of tall letters.

☐ The descenders do not go too far below the baseline.

Add these items to the schedule.

baseball practice on Tuesday at 5:00
art club on Wednesday at 4:00

COLLISION ALERT   Make sure your tall letters do not bump into the descenders above them.

Do your tall letters bump into your descenders?   Yes No

Are your entries legible?   Yes No

52

EVALUATE

After students have evaluated the legibility of their schedule entries, discuss "bumping." Ask what they did to make sure their tall letters did not bump into descenders. (visual, auditory)

On Your Own

Write a schedule of your own for next week.

Monday

Tuesday

Wednesday

Thursday

Friday

EVALUATE

Is your schedule legible?   Yes   No

Will you be able to read it next week?   Yes   No

Ask students to write a journal entry telling what they did last weekend.

COACHING HINT

Provide a small amount of shaving cream, a drop of tempera paint, and a paper plate for each student. Direct students to mix the shaving cream and the paint with their fingertips, then practice the strokes, letters, and joinings you call out. Repeat several times and allow time for students to experiment with various patterns of strokes. (visual, auditory, kinesthetic)

EVALUATE

Have students determine whether their writing is legible. Ask them to check whether their tall letters bump into descenders. Encourage students to practice writing words with tall letters beneath words with descenders, shifting words slightly if necessary. (visual, auditory, kinesthetic)

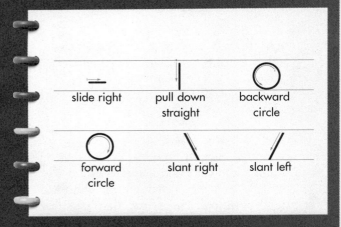

| slide right | pull down straight | backward circle |
| forward circle | slant right | slant left |

Before students begin, review basic strokes for manuscript writing. Remind students that all manuscript letters are formed with these strokes and that manuscript writing is vertical and not slanted to the right. Have students practice the strokes and letterforms. Have them adjust the size of their letters to fit the new writing space. Be sure students adjust the position of the paper for manuscript writing. (visual, auditory, kinesthetic)

The word puzzles on pages 54 and 55 are reproduced on Practice Masters 27 and 28.

Practice Masters 69–76 provide manuscript writing practice.

Use Manuscript for Word Puzzles

When you do word puzzles, you usually write in manuscript. Manuscript letters fit in the puzzle spaces.

Try this clipped-word puzzle. Write the shortened form for each word. The first one is done for you.

WORD	SHORTENED FORM
gymnasium	g y m
gasoline	g a s
teenager	t e e n
submarine	s u b
scramble	s c r a m
champion	c h a m p
hamburger	b u r g e r
taxicab	t a x i
telephone	p h o n e
mathematics	m a t h

Read the letters in the boxes from top to bottom to find the answer to the question.

What kind of writing consists of letters that are not joined?

manuscript

54

EVALUATE

Remind students they are writing for themselves. Ask if they are able to read their puzzle answers. Encourage them to explain why or why not. (visual, auditory)

M MAINTAINING MANUSCRIPT

You may wish to have students do the following activities for reinforcement of manuscript writing.

1. Write their spelling words in manuscript.

2. Prepare a chart or poster in manuscript.

3. Do a crossword puzzle in manuscript.

4. Do a map in manuscript.

5. Write an outline in manuscript.

Solve this antonym crossword puzzle. Write the opposite of each clue word. Use uppercase manuscript letters.

LEGIBLE LETTERS Adjust the size and shape of your letters to fit the writing space.

ACROSS

The opposite of . . .

1. none
3. days
6. even
7. big
9. sweet
10. open
12. same
15. here
17. far
18. sunrise

DOWN

The opposite of . . .

2. found
4. his
5. add
7. first
8. begin
9. finish
11. over
13. back
14. yes
16. her

Crossword grid:
Across: 1. ALL 3. NIGHTS 6. ODD 7. LITTLE 9. SOUR 10. SHUT 12. DIFFERENT 15. THERE 17. NEAR 18. SUNSET
Down: 2. LOST 4. HERS 5. SUBTRACT 7. LAST 8. END 9. STACCATO 11. UNDER 13. FRONT 14. NO 16. THEIR

E V A L U A T E

Did you use uppercase manuscript letters? Yes No

Do your letters fit the writing space? Yes No

55

EVALUATE

Have students focus on size and shape to determine whether their manuscript letters are legible. Discuss whether or not students need to improve legibility. (visual, auditory)

Write Away

Pair students and ask them to use manuscript to create a word search puzzle for classmates to solve. Participate by providing a sample puzzle and challenging a student to solve it.

c f l d o g v b m
k m s p c a t i a
r e g i t q r r b
s k l j h g e d f

COACHING HINT

When is a backward circle used instead of a forward circle? If a circle in a letter comes before the vertical stroke, a backward circle is used, as in **a**. If a vertical stroke in a letter comes before the circle, a forward circle is used, as in **b**. (visual)

JONES RD JAMES RD

Writing for Someone Else

Sometimes you write things for someone else to read. For example, you might write directions to help a new friend get to your house.

What other things might you write for someone else to read?

_____

_____

When you write for someone else, your writing must be legible to the reader.

In the following pages, you will write a note, take a telephone message, and sign an autograph book. As you write, you will focus on uniform slant to help make your writing legible. Later on, you will focus on spacing.

56

UNIT SUMMARY

This unit is the second of three units that link audience and legibility. This page tells students about the content, organization, and focus of the unit. Then students are introduced to the third key to legibility: uniform slant. The lessons that follow have writing activities in which students write for others. Evaluations focus on uniform slant. The primary goal for students is to make their writing legible for someone else.

PREVIEW THE UNIT

Preview the unit with students, calling attention to these features:

- guidelines without a midline and a descender space
- samples of writing to evaluate
- hints about writing with uniform slant
- independent writing activities
- opportunities to work with classmates to evaluate slant and legibility
- a writing activity for manuscript maintenance

Keys to Legibility: Uniform Slant

Now that you are writing smaller, you can concentrate on uniform slant. Your writing will be easier to read if all the letters slant the same way.

Here are some things to do to help you write with uniform slant.

If you are left-handed . . .

Check your paper position.

Pull your downstrokes in the proper direction.

If you are right-handed . . .

Shift your paper.

Now write this sentence. Try to make your slant uniform.

This is uniform slant.

Check your slant.
Draw lines through the slant strokes of the letters.
Your slant should look like

HHHHH, not *AAAA* .

57

PRACTICE MASTERS FOR UNIT 5

- **Use Manuscript for Forms, 29–30**
- **Record of Student's Handwriting Skills, 31**
- **Certificates, 32–34**
- **Write in Spanish, 47–65**
- **Write in Japanese, 66–68**
- **Write in the Content Areas, 69–76**
- **Zaner-Bloser Handwriting Grid, 78**

WRITING FOR SOMEONE ELSE

To provide more opportunities to write for someone else, you may wish to ask students to consider legibility as they write:

- **invitations and greeting cards**
- **awards and announcements**
- **personal business cards**
- **signs and charts**
- **place cards for a special meal**
- **catalog order forms**

MODEL THE WRITING

Point out that in cursive writing all letters slant to the right. To show an example of correct slant, write the word **uniform** on guidelines. Invite a student to check the slant of your writing by drawing lines through the slant strokes of the letters. These lines should be parallel. (visual, auditory, kinesthetic)

EVALUATE

Guide students through the self-evaluation process. Then ask them if they can read their sentences easily. Encourage them to explain why or why not. (visual, auditory)

KEYS TO LEGIBILITY: UNIFORM SLANT

Before students begin, remind them that, in cursive writing, all letters should be slanted to the right. Demonstrate how to write with uniform slant for both left-handed and right-handed students.

- Position your paper correctly.
- Pull the downstrokes in the proper direction.
- Shift your paper to the left as you write.

Left-handed students pull their downstrokes toward the left elbow. Right-handed students pull their downstrokes toward the mid-section.

Invite volunteers to write rows of letters, and have classmates check the slant by drawing lines through the slant strokes of the letters. (visual, auditory, kinesthetic)

Write a Note

Sometimes you write a note to a friend or relative.

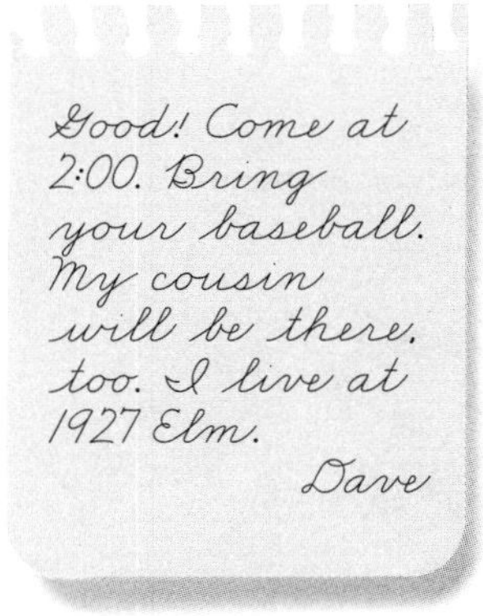

Which note is easier to read? Why?

Write one sentence from Steve's note. As you write, slant the letters the same way. Check the way you hold your pencil and place your paper.

 Check to see if your slant is uniform.
Draw lines through the slant strokes of the letters.
Does your writing have uniform slant?   Yes   No

58

EVALUATE

After students have evaluated their slant, have them describe what they did to make their slant uniform. Ask if their writing is legible. Ask them to explain why or why not. (visual, auditory)

On Your Own

Write a note to a friend. You might share some news,
ask for information, or make plans.

Ask a friend to read and evaluate your writing.
Is the note legible?   Yes   No

59

Ask students to imagine they have gone
on a family vacation. Have them write
a postcard to a friend or a relative,
address it, and then draw a picture of
the vacation spot on the other side.

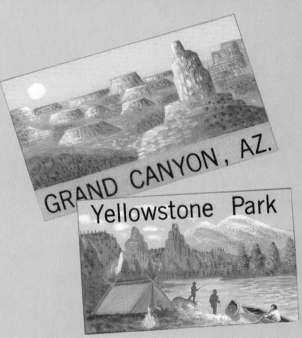

EVALUATE

Pair students and have them discuss how slant has affected the legibility of their writing. Suggest students check the slant of a word by drawing lines through the slant strokes. Encourage them to practice pulling slant strokes in the proper direction. (visual, auditory, kinesthetic)

COACHING HINT

Most errors in slant can be corrected in one of the following ways:

1. Check paper position.

2. Be sure to pull the downstrokes in the proper direction.

3. Remember to shift the writing hand while writing a word and to shift the paper as the writing progresses across the line. (visual, kinesthetic)

Before students begin, remind them that, in cursive writing, all letters should be slanted in the same direction. Review the hints for writing with uniform slant (POSITION, PULL, SHIFT). Help students position their papers correctly and check the direction of their downstrokes. Demonstrate how to shift the paper. (visual, auditory, kinesthetic)

Practice Masters 69–76 provide practice in writing across the curriculum.

Take a Telephone Message

When you take a telephone message, you must write quickly and legibly.

What makes Liza's message legible? Check the true statements.

☐ The size of the letters is correct.

☐ The descenders do not go too far below the baseline.

☐ The slant of the writing is uniform.

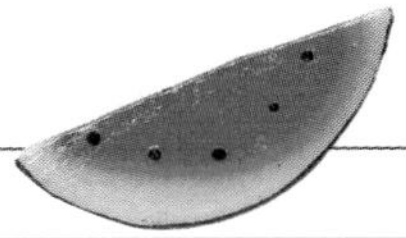

Add the following message to the pad.

Call Mrs. Martinez tonight to arrange a time for your next parent-teacher conference.

POSITION Remember! Check the way
PULL you hold your pencil and
SHIFT place your paper.

*Mom,
Your dental
appointment
will be Fri.
morning at 9:00.
Call if you
can't make it.
Liza*

E V A L U A T E

Check to see if your slant is uniform.

Draw lines through the slant strokes of the letters.

Does your writing have uniform slant?   Yes   No

60

EVALUATE

After students have evaluated their slant, ask if their writing is legible. Ask them to explain why or why not. (visual, auditory)

On Your Own

Imagine that you listened to the following message for a friend named Elana. Write it down for her. Include the caller's name, the day and time of the call, and important details.

Hi, Elana! This is Coach Andrews. How are you this rainy Thursday? It is now 6:00 P.M. I am calling to remind you that we will be taking a team picture tomorrow at 5:00 P.M. Please wear your uniform and bring your hat. If it rains, we will take the picture on Saturday.

E V A L U A T E

Ask a friend to read and evaluate your writing.
Is the message legible?   Yes   No

EVALUATE

Pair students and have them discuss how slant has affected the legibility of their writing. Suggest students look at the slant of one group of letters in their words (for example, overcurve letters) and check if the slant is uniform. Encourage students to write several rows of letters, using the hints for writing with uniform slant. (visual, auditory, kinesthetic)

Write Away

Ask students to imagine that a neighbor has stopped by to invite the family to a garage sale. Have them take a message and write what the neighbor has to say. Tell them to include the neighbor's name, the day, the starting and ending times of the sale, and a few items that will be sold.

COACHING HINT

Holding the writing instrument correctly has an obvious effect on handwriting quality. Students having difficulty with the conventional method of holding the writing instrument may wish to try an alternate method: placing the pen or pencil between the first and second fingers. (visual, kinesthetic)

KEYS TO LEGIBILITY:
UNIFORM SLANT

Before students begin, remind them that, in cursive writing, all letters should be slanted in the same direction. Point out that uniform slant is especially important when there are no writing lines. Tell students to concentrate on both keeping their slant uniform and keeping their writing straight. Have students sign their names on an unlined sheet of paper and evaluate the slant. (visual, auditory, kinesthetic)

Practice Masters 47–65 provide practice in writing in Spanish. Practice Masters 66–68 provide practice in writing in Japanese.

Sign an Autograph Book

Here are some ways to sign an autograph book.

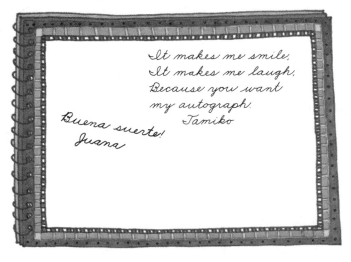

Draw lines to check the slant of one autograph.

Is the slant uniform?   Yes   No

Write this saying. Add your signature.

Think of Ted and think of Bea.
Don't forget to think of me!

Does your writing have uniform slant?   Yes   No

62

EVALUATE

After students have evaluated their slant, ask if their writing is legible. Ask them to explain why or why not. (visual, auditory)

On Your Own

Sign these autograph book pages. Include a
saying and your signature on each page.

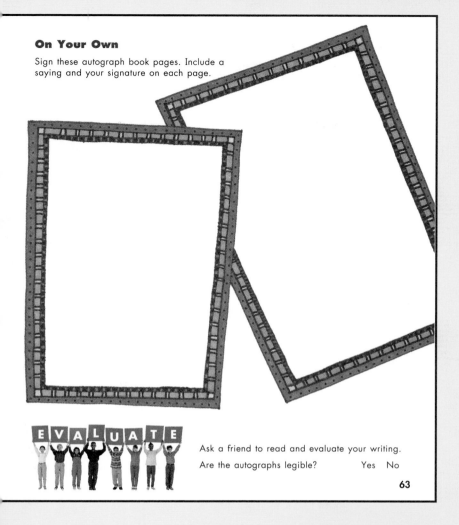

E V A L U A T E

Ask a friend to read and evaluate your writing.

Are the autographs legible?　　Yes　No

63

EVALUATE

Pair students and have them discuss how slant has affected the legibility of their writing. Suggest students check the slant of a word by drawing lines through the slant strokes. Encourage them to write a word or verse on notebook paper, using the hints for writing with uniform slant. (visual, auditory, kinesthetic)

Ask students to imagine they are a famous person. Encourage them to write and sign a note from that person.

See you in Washington, George

COACHING HINT

Give each student a card on which one of the basic strokes is written. Tell students to write that basic stroke on paper and to write all the uppercase and lowercase letters that have that stroke. If time permits, have students trade cards and do the same with a different basic stroke. (visual, kinesthetic)

MANUSCRIPT MAINTENANCE

Carol

Before students begin, review the keys to legibility for manuscript writing: size and shape, slant, and spacing. Encourage students to follow these suggestions.

- Position the paper correctly.
- Pull the downstrokes in the proper direction.
- Shift the paper as your writing fills the space.

Right-handed students should pull downstrokes toward the midsection. Left-handed students should pull downstrokes toward the left elbow. Guide students in evaluating vertical quality. (visual, auditory, kinesthetic)

The forms on pages 64–65 are reproduced on Practice Masters 29–30.

Practice Masters 69–76 provide manuscript writing practice.

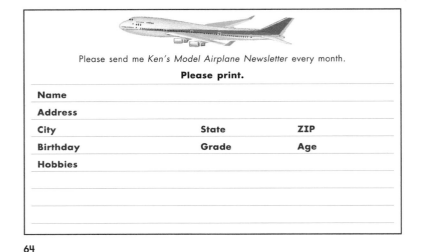

Use Manuscript for Forms

On most forms, you see the words **Please print**. Use manuscript to fill out the order form below with the following information:

Jonathan Jackson

455 Westfield Road

Knoxville, TN 37901

Birthday: January 1

Grade: 4

Age: 9

Hobbies: building model airplanes, playing soccer

Please send me *Ken's Model Airplane Newsletter* every month.

Please print.

Name		
Address		
City	State	ZIP
Birthday	Grade	Age
Hobbies		

64

EVALUATE

Remind students they are writing for someone else. Guide them through the evaluation process. Ask them to check for correct vertical quality in manuscript. (visual, auditory)

MAINTAINING MANUSCRIPT

Students should remember that the Keys to Legibility apply to the manuscript maintenance activities. It is recommended that teachers review their application regularly, since students will have frequent situations that require manuscript writing. The difference in the slant (vertical quality) of manuscript is the most obvious variation, and students need to be able to make this adjustment readily. By visualizing parallel vertical lines over the pull down straight strokes of manuscript letters, the student can quickly evaluate the vertical quality of manuscript writing.

On Your Own

Join a book club. Fill out the side of the form that asks about you and your interests. Please print.

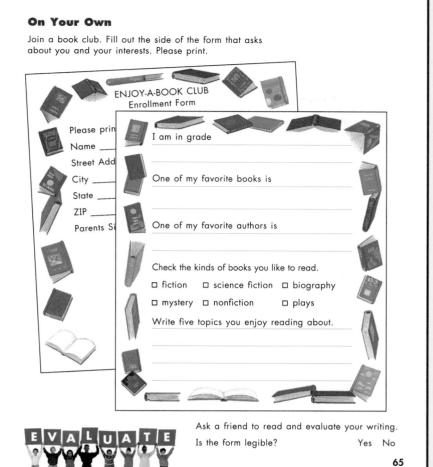

ENJOY-A-BOOK CLUB
Enrollment Form

Please prin
Name
Street Add
City
State
ZIP
Parents Si

I am in grade

_____

One of my favorite books is

_____

One of my favorite authors is

_____

Check the kinds of books you like to read.
☐ fiction   ☐ science fiction   ☐ biography
☐ mystery   ☐ nonfiction   ☐ plays

Write five topics you enjoy reading about.

_____
_____
_____

Ask a friend to read and evaluate your writing.
Is the form legible?   Yes   No

65

EVALUATE

Pair students and have them discuss the legibility of their application forms. Encourage students to make suggestions for improving legibility. (visual, auditory)

Provide various experiences in filling out forms and applications in the classroom. You may include health forms, order forms from catalogs, and applications for jobs and organizations.

COACHING HINT

Practicing pull down straight strokes at the chalkboard is a good method for improving poor strokes. Place sets of two dots about six inches apart to mark the starting and stopping points of each vertical stroke. (visual, kinesthetic)

Before You Go On . . .

Before You Go On . . .

Huh?

Writing for Publication

Sometimes you write things that many people will read. For example, you might write a notice about a science fair for all the students at your school.

What else might you write for many people to read?

_____

_____

When you write for publication, your writing must be legible to many different readers. It may be helpful to write a first draft before writing a final draft in your best handwriting.

In the following pages, you will write selections for a group anthology and a class magazine. As you write, you will focus on correct spacing to help make your writing legible.

66

UNIT SUMMARY

This unit is the last of three units that link audience and legibility. This page tells students about the content, organization, and focus of the unit. Then students are introduced to the fourth key to legibility: correct spacing. The lessons that follow have writing activities in which students work together to write for publication. Evaluations focus on correct spacing. The primary goal for students is to make their writing legible for others.

PREVIEW THE UNIT

Preview the unit with students, calling attention to these features:

- guidelines without a midline and a descender space
- four-page lessons involving five steps in the writing process
- class, group, and individual activities
- hints for achieving correct spacing
- opportunities to evaluate size and shape, slant, and spacing
- a writing activity for manuscript maintenance

Keys to Legibility: Correct Spacing

You have been writing smaller with uniform slant. Now look at spacing. Your writing will be easier to read if the spacing between letters, words, and sentences is correct.

Between Letters There should be enough space for O.

handwriting

Between Words There should be enough space for \.

The spacing between words is correct.

Between Sentences There should be enough space for O.

Spacing is important. O So is slant.

Write the following sentences.

This is legible. The slant is uniform. The spacing is correct.

Is there space for O between letters? Yes No
Is there space for \ between words? Yes No
Is there space for O between sentences?
Yes No

MODEL THE WRITING

To show an example of correct spacing, write the following sentences on guidelines: **My writing is legible. The spacing is correct.** Invite volunteers to check the spacing by drawing ovals between letters, drawing slanted lines between words, and writing uppercase **O**s between sentences. (visual, auditory, kinesthetic)

EVALUATE

Guide students through the self-evaluation process. Then ask them if they can read their sentences easily. Encourage them to explain why or why not. (visual, auditory)

PRACTICE MASTERS FOR UNIT 6

- Record of Student's Handwriting Skills, 31
- Certificates, 32–34
- Write in Spanish, 47–65
- Write in Japanese, 66–68
- Write in the Content Areas, 69–76
- Zaner-Bloser Handwriting Grid, 78

WRITING FOR PUBLICATION

To provide more opportunities to write for publication, you may wish to ask students to consider legibility as they write:

- letters to the editor
- storybooks for younger children
- book and movie reviews
- travel brochures
- advertisements
- informative posters

BRAINSTORMING

Have students use the following four steps for brainstorming. Remind them that only one member of the group should talk at a time.

> Say everything that you think of.

> Write down every idea as it is said.

> Keep going until there are no more ideas.

> Choose the group's subject by voting.

Practice Masters 69–76 are available for use with this unit.

Write for an Anthology

An anthology is a collection of writings. It may contain original writings or the writings of others.

Follow these suggestions for putting together an anthology with your group.

I. Prewriting

Begin by thinking about a topic for your group's anthology. **Brainstorm** with your group to add ideas to the list below. Write legibly so everyone can read the list.

> *poems*
> *songs*
> *sports*
> *recipes*
> *limericks*

Look back at the list and decide what your group will do. What is the subject of your group's anthology?

EVALUATE

Have students evaluate the legibility of their brainstorming notes. Ask if they can read their notes now. Suggest they cross out and rewrite any words they might find hard to read later. (visual, auditory, kinesthetic)

HANDWRITING AND THE WRITING PROCESS

Invite students to preview the lesson for the five steps in writing for publication:

Discuss the relationship between handwriting and the writing process. Point out that students' best handwriting is necessary only for the final stage, Publishing. However, legible writing is important throughout the process. Ask students to give examples of how legible writing might make each step of the writing process easier and more efficient.

Now use this form to **plan** what your contribution to the group anthology will be. Make sure you will be able to read your notes later.

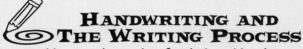

Notes

Date: _____

Subject of my group's anthology: _____

What I want to look for or write about: _____

_____

_____

_____

What I will do next: _____

_____

_____

_____

What have you decided to write for your anthology? _____

_____

EVALUATE

Ask students to evaluate the legibility of their planning notes, reminding them to keep in mind that the notes are for their own use. Suggest that students cross out and rewrite any words they might find hard to read later. (visual, auditory, kinesthetic)

HANDWRITING AND THE WRITING PROCESS

During prewriting, students plan for their writing by making notes, lists, and webs. "Sloppy" prewriting work may cause confusion that remains throughout the writing process, but easy-to-read notes and webs smooth the way for students, teachers, and writing partners.

As students complete their brainstorming lists and planning notes, discuss the possible confusion illegible writing could cause for students, teachers, and classmates. Ask why legible writing might be especially important for prewriting tasks such as taking research notes or serving as a group secretary.

Cooperative and collaborative learning create an ideal environment for student interaction. Organize groups so that students of differing strengths join forces to work together. Assist by actively monitoring and advising each group, setting performance time limits, and keeping each team on track.

KEYS TO LEGIBILITY: CORRECT SPACING

Spacing

Before students write their first draft, display an example of correct spacing between letters, words, and sentences.

Between Letters There should be enough space for O.

Between Words There should be enough space for \.

Between Sentences There should be enough space for O.

Provide opportunities for students to write two or more sentences and to check the spacing between letters, words, and sentences. (auditory, visual, kinesthetic)

COACHING HINT
Remind students to shift their paper as they write to keep spacing consistent. (visual, kinesthetic)

2. Drafting
Begin your first draft. If your writing is not original, be sure to include the author's name. Your draft will be easier to revise and edit if you write legibly.

Is there space for O between letters? Yes No

Is there space for \ between words? Yes No

Is there space for O between sentences?

Yes No

70

EVALUATE
After students have evaluated their spacing, ask if their writing is legible. Ask them to explain why or why not. (visual, auditory)

HANDWRITING AND THE WRITING PROCESS
Students' best handwriting isn't necessary for a first draft. In fact, concentrating too much on handwriting may take students' attention away from the content of their writing. However, a "sloppy" draft makes revising and editing more difficult. As students develop a consciousness about legibility, their writing will be fluent **and** easy to read.

3. Revising

Read your first draft and mark any changes you want to make. You may ask a partner to help you.

4. Editing

Check for errors in spelling, punctuation, and capitalization. Then answer the questions below to edit your handwriting. You may ask a partner to help you.

Did you write in the new size?	Yes	No
Are all your tall letters the same size?	Yes	No
Are your short letters half the size of your tall letters?	Yes	No
Did you avoid collisions?	Yes	No
Does your writing have uniform slant?	Yes	No
Is there space for $\mathcal{O}$ between letters?	Yes	No
Is there space for $\setminus$ between words?	Yes	No
Is there space for $\mathcal{O}$ between sentences?	Yes	No
Do you think your writing is easy to read?	Yes	No
Do you think it will be legible to many people?	Yes	No

5. Publishing

Use your best handwriting as you make a clean, neat copy of your work. Then follow these steps to publish your anthology with your group:

- Choose a title.
- Design a cover.
- Add illustrations.
- Assemble the pages.
- Make copies and share with others.

71

EVALUATE

Have students determine whether their writing is ready for publication. Ask them to use the checklist on page 71 to identify any areas where improvement is needed. (visual, auditory, kinesthetic)

HANDWRITING AND THE WRITING PROCESS

Along with spelling, punctuation, and other language mechanics, thinking about legibility should always be part of the editing stage of the writing process. A list of questions related to the Keys to Legibility (size and shape, slant, and spacing), like the one on page 71, is a useful tool to incorporate into students' regular editing routine. You may wish to work as a class to devise editing symbols to use for marking spots in a draft where handwriting needs to be improved.

Publishing always requires students' best handwriting. Neat, legible writing shows courtesy to readers. It makes a good first impression, and it helps ensure that readers will understand the writer's message. Encourage students to do their personal best as they make a final copy of their work, making sure to incorporate all the changes they marked during revising and editing.

Invite students to compile an anthology of celebrity autographs. Students can work in groups to determine the kinds of autographs to collect and to develop a plan for acquiring the signatures. You might suggest that students organize their collections around a profession, such as sports, or an event, such as a space shuttle mission.

good spacing

Before students begin, review the keys to legibility for manuscript writing: size and shape, slant, and spacing. Show an example of correct spacing between letters, words, and sentences. Remind students that letters and words that are too close together or too far apart make writing difficult to read. Provide opportunities for them to practice good spacing. (visual, auditory, kinesthetic)

Practice Masters 69–76 provide manuscript writing practice.

Use Manuscript for Posters

You can have fun with manuscript letters and create eye-catching posters using picture words. Here are some examples of picture words. Each word looks like its meaning.

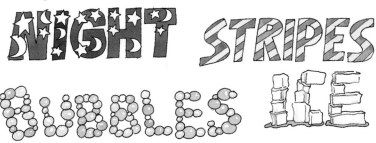

Use your imagination. Create some picture words of your own.

72

EVALUATE

Remind students they are writing for publication. Encourage them to think about how others might react to their picture words. (visual, auditory)

 ### MAINTAINING MANUSCRIPT

To emphasize the need for manuscript, discuss situations that require manuscript writing. If possible, provide samples of job applications, subscription cards, test forms, tax returns, and bank forms as examples of the need for manuscript writing. Allow students to practice filling out a form requiring name, address, age, and phone number. Discuss potential problems with these forms if the manuscript is illegible, and role-play such situations.

On Your Own

Design a poster for something that is going to happen, or that you wish would happen, at your school. Be creative and make your poster eye-catching.

EVALUATE

In designing your poster, what did you do to catch the reader's attention?

73

EVALUATE

Invite students to share their posters with classmates and to respond to their classmates' posters. Encourage discussion of what is most effective in each student's presentation and use of space. (visual, auditory)

Write Away

Ask students to design a travel poster for a place they would like to visit. Participate by having available several travel posters from well-known tourist spots.

COACHING HINT

To reinforce manuscript writing, you may wish to have students use manuscript to prepare invitations to parties, send holiday greetings, and label maps and diagrams. (visual, kinesthetic)

Remind students to follow these guidelines when they work with a writing partner.

> Listen carefully to your partner.

> Give positive feedback first.

> Ask questions that will help your partner.

> Be honest and kind when making suggestions about your partner's work.

Write for a Class Magazine

A class magazine is a great place for sharing things that interest you and your classmates. It may include different kinds of writing.

Follow these suggestions for putting together a class magazine.

I. Prewriting

Begin by choosing an assignment that interests you. The list below shows some types of articles you could write. Discuss the list with a partner, then **brainstorm** ideas of your own.

news articles   poems
stories   jokes
book reviews   riddles
magazine reviews

What kind of article will you write? Explain your choice.

_____

_____

_____

EVALUATE

Have students evaluate the legibility of their brainstorming notes. Ask if they can read their notes now. Suggest they cross out and rewrite any words they might find hard to read later. (visual, auditory, kinesthetic)

HANDWRITING AND THE WRITING PROCESS

Invite students to preview the lesson for the five steps in writing for publication:

Discuss the relationship between handwriting and the writing process. Point out that students' best handwriting is necessary only for the final stage, Publishing. However, legible writing is important throughout the process. Ask students to give examples of how legible writing might make each step of the writing process easier and more efficient.

Now use the form below to **plan** your article. Make sure you will be able to read your notes later.

Notes

Date: _____

Kind of article: _____

Subject of my article: _____

What I already know: _____

What I need to find out: _____

Think of an interesting title for your article.
Write it below.

_____

EVALUATE

Ask students to evaluate the legibility of their planning notes, reminding them to keep in mind that the notes are for their own use. Suggest that students cross out and rewrite any words they might find hard to read later. (visual, auditory, kinesthetic)

HANDWRITING AND THE WRITING PROCESS

During prewriting, students plan for their writing by making notes, lists, and webs. "Sloppy" prewriting work may cause confusion that remains throughout the writing process, but easy-to-read notes and webs smooth the way for students, teachers, and writing partners.

As students complete their brainstorming and planning notes, discuss the possible confusion illegible writing could cause for students, teachers, and classmates. Ask why legible writing might be especially important for prewriting tasks such as taking research notes or serving as a group secretary.

COACHING HINT: CLASSROOM MANAGEMENT

When pairing students for brainstorming, choose partners whose strengths complement each other's. Actively serve as an adviser to each pair. Assist by giving additional explanations and setting performance time limits. Remind students to use the four brainstorming steps shown on page 68.

KEYS TO LEGIBILITY: CORRECT SPACING

Before students write their first draft, remind them to pay attention to spacing.

Between Letters There should be enough space for O.

Between Words There should be enough space for \.

Between Sentences There should be enough space for O.

Provide opportunities for students to write sentence pairs and to check the spacing between letters, words, and sentences. (auditory, visual, kinesthetic)

2. Drafting

Begin your first draft. Your draft will be easier to revise and edit if you write legibly.

Is there space for O between letters?   Yes No

Is there space for \ between words?   Yes No

Is there space for O between sentences? Yes No

EVALUATE

After students have evaluated their spacing, ask if their writing is legible. Ask them to explain why or why not. (visual, auditory)

HANDWRITING AND THE WRITING PROCESS

Students' best handwriting isn't necessary for a first draft. In fact, concentrating too much on handwriting may take students' attention away from the content of their writing. However, a "sloppy" draft makes revising and editing more difficult. As students develop a consciousness about legibility, their writing will be fluent **and** easy to read.

3. Revising

Read your first draft and mark any changes you want to make. You may ask a partner to help you.

4. Editing

Check for errors in spelling, punctuation, and capitalization. Then answer the questions below to edit your handwriting. You may ask a partner to help you.

Did you write in the new size?	Yes	No
Are all your tall letters the same size?	Yes	No
Are your short letters half the size of your tall letters?	Yes	No
Did you avoid collisions?	Yes	No
Does your writing have uniform slant?	Yes	No
Is there space for ⵔ between letters?	Yes	No
Is there space for ⟍ between words?	Yes	No
Is there space for ⵔ between sentences?	Yes	No
Do you think your writing is easy to read?	Yes	No
Do you think it will be legible to many people?	Yes	No

5. Publishing

Use your best handwriting as you make a clean, neat copy of your article. Then work with your class to publish your magazine.

- Choose a name.
- Design a cover.
- Add illustrations.
- Assemble the pages.
- Make copies and share with others.

77

EVALUATE

Have students determine whether their writing is ready for publication. Ask them to use the checklist on page 77 to identify any areas where improvement is needed. (visual, auditory, kinesthetic)

HANDWRITING AND THE WRITING PROCESS

Along with spelling, punctuation, and other language mechanics, thinking about legibility should always be part of the editing stage of the writing process. A list of questions related to the Keys to Legibility (size and shape, slant, and spacing), like the one on page 77, is a useful tool to incorporate into students' regular editing routine. You may wish to work as a class to devise editing symbols to use for marking spots in a draft where handwriting needs to be improved.

Publishing always requires students' best handwriting. Neat, legible writing shows courtesy to readers. It makes a good first impression, and it helps ensure that readers will understand the writer's message. Encourage students to do their personal best as they make a final copy of their work, making sure to incorporate all the changes they marked during revising and editing.

Ask students to write about special days or events in their lives. Then have them put together a class anthology by choosing a title, designing a cover, adding illustrations, assembling the pages, and making copies.

Certificates of Progress *should be awarded to those students who show notable handwriting progress and* Certificates of Excellence *to those who progress to the top levels of handwriting proficiency.*

Remind students that on page 7 they wrote lines from this poem as a pretest and evaluated their handwriting. Have students write the same lines for the posttest. As they write, tell students to use correct letter size and shape, uniform slant, and correct spacing. (visual, auditory, kinesthetic)

Posttest

It's Dark in Here

by Shel Silverstein

I am writing these poems
From inside a lion,
And it's rather dark in here.
So please excuse the handwriting
Which may not be too clear.
But this afternoon by the lion's cage
I'm afraid I got too near.
And I'm writing these lines
From inside a lion,
And it's rather dark in here.

On your paper, write the first five lines of this poem in your best cursive handwriting.

E V A L U A T E

Is your writing legible?   Yes   No

78

EVALUATE

Have students use the keys to legibility to evaluate their handwriting. Suggest they compare this writing with their writing on the pretest, and discuss how their writing has changed. If feasible, meet individually with students to help them assess their progress. (visual, auditory)

Record of Student's Handwriting Skills

Cursive

	Needs Improvement	Shows Mastery		Needs Improvement	Shows Mastery
Sits correctly	☐	☐	Writes the undercurve to undercurve joining	☐	☐
Holds pencil correctly	☐	☐	Writes the undercurve to downcurve joining	☐	☐
Positions paper correctly	☐	☐			
Writes numerals **1–10**	☐	☐	Writes the undercurve to overcurve joining	☐	☐
Writes undercurve letters: **i, t, u, w**	☐	☐	Writes the overcurve to undercurve joining	☐	☐
Writes undercurve letters: **r, s, p, j**	☐	☐	Writes the overcurve to downcurve joining	☐	☐
Writes downcurve letters: **a, c, d, q, g, o**	☐	☐	Writes the overcurve to overcurve joining	☐	☐
Writes overcurve letters: **n, m, x, y, z, v**	☐	☐	Writes the checkstroke to undercurve joining	☐	☐
Writes letters with loops: **e, l, h, k, f, b**	☐	☐	Writes the checkstroke to downcurve joining	☐	☐
Writes downcurve letters: **A, C, E, O**	☐	☐	Writes the checkstroke to overcurve joining	☐	☐
Writes curve forward letters: **N, M, K, H**	☐	☐	Writes in the new size	☐	☐
Writes curve forward letters: **U, Y, Z**	☐	☐	Writes with correct size and shape	☐	☐
Writes curve forward letters: **V, X, W**	☐	☐	Writes with uniform slant	☐	☐
Writes doublecurve letters: **T, F**	☐	☐	Writes with correct spacing	☐	☐
Writes overcurve letters: **I, J, Q**	☐	☐	Writes legibly for self	☐	☐
			Writes legibly for someone else	☐	☐
			Writes legibly for publication	☐	☐
Writes letters with loops: **G, S, L, D**	☐	☐	Regularly checks written work for legibility	☐	☐
Writes undercurve-slant letters: **P, R, B**	☐	☐			

79

The form on page 79 is reproduced on Practice Master 31.

COACHING HINT

If a student needs improvement, reevaluate his or her writing following practice over a period of time. Invite the student to share in the evaluation.

EVALUATE

This chart provides a place for you to record the student's handwriting progress. The chart lists the essential skills in the program. After each skill has been practiced and evaluated, you can indicate whether the student *Shows Mastery* or *Needs Improvement* by checking the appropriate box.

Shows Mastery Mastery of written letterforms is achieved when the student writes the letters using correct basic strokes. Compare the student's written letterforms with the letter models. Keep in mind the keys to legibility (size and shape, slant, and spacing) when evaluating letters, numerals, punctuation marks, words, and sentences.

Needs Improvement If a student has not mastered a skill, provide additional basic instruction and practice. To improve letterforms, have the student practice writing the letter in isolation and within words and sentences. Reinforce instruction through activities geared to the student's modality strengths. When mastery of the skill is achieved, check *Shows Mastery*.

Index